CSP II

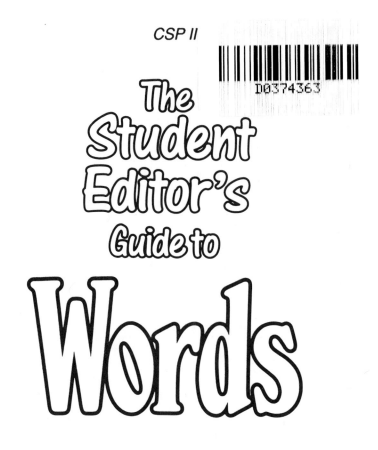

The
Student
Editor's
Guide to
Words

Ruth Scott

 EDUCATIONAL PUBLISHING COMPANY
A DIVISION OF CANADA PUBLISHING CORPORATION
TORONTO ONTARIO CANADA

Canadian Cataloguing in Publication Data

Scott, Ruth
 The student editor's guide to words
 Includes bibliographical references.
 ISBN 0-7715-1578-2
 1. English language—Orthography and spelling—
 Juvenile literature. I. Title.
 PE1143.S36   1991   428.1   C90-095916-9

Cover/text design: Michael Gray/*First Image*
Illustrator: Emmanuel Lopez/*Crackers*
Editorial Team: Jeff Siamon, Carol Waldock

ISBN: 0-7715-1578-2

3 4 5 6 7 KRD 99 98 97 96 95

Written, Printed, and Bound in Canada

Gage Educational Publishing Company wishes to thank the following educators for their evaluation and helpful advice:

Margaret Davies
Centennial Middle School
Halton Board of Education

Ian McKay
Vancouver School District No. 39

Susan Ireland
Maplehurst School
Halton Board of Education

Linda Perrin
School District No. 20
Saint John, New Brunswick

Jill Johnson
The Lakehead Board of Education

Bill Prentice
Swift Current School Division
 No. 94

Glen Kirkland
Edmonton Catholic School
District No. 7

Carolyn Reist
Halton Board of Education

Pauline Leslie
Stewarttown Middle School
Halton Board of Education

Linda Young
School District No. 20
Saint John, New Brunswick

For Wilf, Casey, and Lindsay

To The Student

Speling is importent for cleer and acurite comunicasion. Poor speling maks it dificult for reeder's to understand the thots and detales in a peece of riting.

Let's try that again!!

Spelling is important for clear and accurate communication. Poor spelling makes it difficult for readers to understand the thoughts and details in a piece of writing.

The first version of the paragraph above is unedited, and, as you would have noticed, has many spelling errors. Did these mistakes make it more difficult for you to concentrate on the meaning of the paragraph?

Poorly edited writing suggests to the reader that the author doesn't care enough about the piece to make it appear correct. For better or worse, many people will judge your writing by how many spelling errors there are. How do you think an employer feels when a job application has many spelling errors? If you wish to have your writing taken seriously, it's important to be able to spell accurately.

Becoming a good speller, however, doesn't happen overnight. Researchers have found that people pass through many stages before they are able to spell words accurately on a regular basis.

Understanding the way words are spelled in English isn't always an easy task, because many of these words are borrowed from other languages. That's why words such as *limousine* (French), *typhoon* (Chinese), and *yacht* (Dutch) seem so difficult to spell. Also, in English, words are not always spelled the way they sound. Silent letters, as in knowledge, yolk, rhyme, and biscuit, make it necessary to remember how a word looks as well as how it sounds.

I hope **The Student Editor's Guide to Words** will not only help you become a better and a more confident speller, but make you appreciate all the many interesting *words* in the English language.

Good luck!

Ruth Scott

Table Of Contents

Chapter 3   Editing/Proofreading 75

Chapter 4   Using the Dictionary and Thesaurus 92

Chapter 8   Further Investigations 195

How This Book is Organized

Table of Contents

CHAPTER 1: Spelling Strategies

Here are a variety of strategies which you can use to spell almost any word in the English language. You can practise each strategy with words you need to learn.

CHAPTER 2: Spelling Patterns

This chapter outlines at least thirty major spelling patterns in English. The patterns are explained using many examples.

- Other words showing the same patterns are listed in **Chapter 7: Word Lists**.
- Activities can be found in **Chapter 8: Further Investigations** to help you to practise each pattern.

CHAPTER 3: Editing/Proofreading

Chapter 3 offers a number of aids to help you improve your proofreading skills.

- A list of proofreading strategies on page 76.
- A proofreader's checklist on page 77.
- A number of proofreading passages are also included so that you can practise proofreading for specific types of spelling errors.

CHAPTER 4: Using the Dictionary and Thesaurus

This chapter explains how to use these two important editing tools.

- A dictionary can give you more than just the correct spelling and meaning of a word.
- A thesaurus is very useful for providing synonyms for overly used words.

CHAPTER 5: Language Alive

Words can be fun! Try these activities and word games. They not only will show you how interesting the English language is, but they will help you become a better speller and use words more effectively.

CHAPTERS 6 and 7: Spelling Demons and Word Lists

It is important to apply the spelling strategies and patterns you learn in this handbook to words which you feel are necessary for you to spell.

- A list of *The 200 Most Commonly Misspelled Words* is found on page 131.
- Look up hundreds of examples of words which fit certain spelling patterns, and which may be of interest to you.

CHAPTER 8: Further Investigations

In this chapter there are activities for each of the spelling and word patterns found in *Chapter 2: Spelling Patterns*. A "cross–reference" chart will help you find more information for each word pattern.

BIBLIOGRAPHY

- You can use the Bibliography on page 216 for further study.

INDEX

If you cannot find what you want in the *Table of Contents*, look it up in the *Index*. All the patterns, strategies, and activities are listed in alphabetical order.

How To Use This Book

The Student Editor's Guide to Words is not a spelling text. You are not expected to begin at page 1 and work your way to the last chapter. Instead, this is a handbook for you to use while you are writing and editing.

Spend some time looking carefully at the **Table of Contents**. You will see that the book is filled with useful information to help you improve as a speller. Then flip through the book, stopping at pages which capture your interest. The more often you explore the contents of the book, the more useful it will be as a personal resource for you.

LEARNING SUGGESTIONS

Here are some suggestions on how to use this book. Maybe you can think of others.

A *You and your teacher notice that the drafts of your writing have many errors in the use of contractions.*

- Look through the **Table of Contents**. In ***Chapter 2: Spelling Patterns***, you will notice that *Contractions* are discussed, on page 39. When you look up *Contractions*, you will find an explanation of some of the rules, as well as many examples.

- After you feel you understand the rules for *Contractions*, practise using them in ***Chapter 8: Further Investigations***, on page 204.

- Then you might want to test your ability to spot the correct and incorrect spelling of *Contractions* by correcting the passage in ***Chapter 3: Editing/Proofreading***, on page 85.

- Look at other examples of *Contractions* in ***Chapter 7: Word Lists***, on page 157.

- Now go back to your writing draft and correct any errors in *Contractions* you have made.

B *You have been asked to study a list of personal spelling words. In trying to learn your words, you have made a number of incorrect guesses.*

- Go to ***Chapter 1: Spelling Strategies***. Use a variety of the suggested strategies to study the words. Try working with a partner or group of friends to find the best study method for each word.

- Next, consider having a partner give you a trial dictation of the words. Notice the specific letters in each word which give you difficulty. Try another strategy for learning each word.

- Keep a record of the words which you have misspelled. Enter them in your Personal Dictionary.

- Think about the spelling strategies which help you to spell words correctly. Remember to use them in the future when editing your writing.

Of course, there are many other interesting ways to use this handbook:
- use the *Word Lists* to make up word games;
- take ideas from *Language Alive* and add them to your writing;
- increase your understanding of the wealth of information found in a dictionary or thesaurus.

Self–analysis Checklist

Here is a list of the types of spelling errors most frequently made by students. Use this list to guide your proofreading during the editing stage of writing. The page numbers will help you find these patterns in this handbook.

	Spelling Patterns	Word Lists	Investi– gations	Proof– reading Passages
Long vowel patterns:				
long /ā/: ai, ay, eigh	28	139	196	
long /ē/: ee, y, ea, ie, i	28	139	196	78
long /ī/: igh	28	140	196	
long /ō/: oa, ow, o	29	140	197	
long /ü/: ui, oo, ew	29	141	197	
Diphthongs /ou/, /oi/	30	142	197	
R–influenced vowels: /ėr/	30	143	198	
Variations on consonant spellings:				
/sh/ and /ch/	31	145	198	

Chapter 1
Spelling Strategies

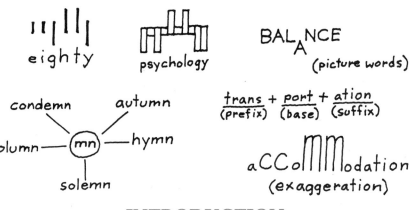

INTRODUCTION

What strategies do you use to spell a new word?

Perhaps you try to sound the word out, or break it into syllables. Do you look at the word carefully and make note of silent letters or unusual letter combinations? Do you think of tricks for remembering the difficult parts of the word?

The following pages suggest many strategies for learning to spell new words. By using many of these techniques you will be able to study words better and spell them correctly.

Combine these study strategies with the spelling patterns and rules in Chapter 2, and you are sure to become a more competent speller.

STRATEGY # 1

Leaving blanks for misspelled letters

A Compare your spelling of the word with the correct spelling.

1. Recopy the parts of the word you have spelled correctly.
2. Leave blank spaces for the letters which were incorrect.

Correct	Incorrect =	Remember
famous	famus	fam_us
anything	enything	_nything
repetition	repitision	rep_ti_ion
because	becuse	bec_use
Saturday	Saterday	Sat_rday

B Focus on learning the correct letters to fit each blank. Here are some ideas to try.

1. Fill in the blanks using a different colour of ink or go over these letters with a "highlighting" pen.

   famous

2. Exaggerate the size of the letters in the blanks.

repEtiTion

3. Think of a "trick" to remember the difficult letters.

Sat_rday: U love SatUrday

4. Link the word with others which share the same spelling pattern.

STRATEGY # 2

Remembering visual features of words

A It is important to be able to remember the exact letters in a word and to record these letters in the correct order. There are a number of approaches which can help you to remember the visual features of words that you find difficult to spell.

1. Gradually leave out more and more spaces until you are writing the whole word.

necessary
necessary
necessary
necessary
necessary
necessary
necessary
necessary
necessary
necessary

2. Stroke or draw the shape of the word. Some learners remember shapes more easily than letters.

hypothesis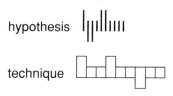

technique

3. Break the word into syllables. Find the word in a dictionary if you are not sure how to divide it.

con · trov · er · sial

4. Use wooden or plastic alphabet squares available in commercial games to spell the word you wish to learn. Scramble the letters, then put them in the correct order and copy the word.

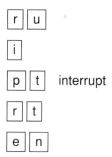

interrupt

5. Write each syllable on a blank card. Scramble the cards, then sort them and copy the word.

6. Create mental pictures to help you remember difficult parts of a word.

We had an argument about the stick of gum
I pursued my stolen purse.

STRATEGY # 3

Word pictures

A It sometimes helps to remember a word by writing it in a way that shows its meaning.

Snake SCARY CA$HIER

POPCORN

ZEBRA

LOOK ınFLATION

DIVISION

B Here are some others to try:

balloon	giraffe	separate	duplicate
forgetful	escalator	shatter	iceberg
toboggan	boomerang	limousine	astronaut
tornado	gravity	infinity	

STRATEGY # 4

Mnemonic devices

A Some words have letter combinations that are very difficult to remember. It may help to think of "tricks" for recalling these letters. Such "tricks" are called **mnemonics** (pronounced *ni mon'iks*).

Raspberry	Autumn	Fascinating
Raspberries are prickly to pick.	November is the last month of autumn.	Science is a fascinating subject.

Exhaust	Accident	Dessert
I was exhausted from the heat and humidity.	Cars cause accidents.	I had a strawberry sundae for dessert.

B Mnemonics work best when you create them yourself. Can you think of helpful mnemonics for some of these words?

broccoli	accommodation	lunar	anxiety
friend	embarrassing	campaign	because
awkward	beautiful	people	salmon
argument	necessary	stubborn	canoe
restaurant	disastrous	parliament	exaggerate

✓ *Mnemonic* devices will often help in remembering the **Spelling Demons** on pages 130–135.

STRATEGY # 5

Pronouncing words clearly

A Words are often misspelled because they are not pronounced clearly in everyday speech. Try to pronounce words carefully so that you hear each sound.

library	*not*	libary
probably	*not*	probly
surprise	*not*	suprise
February	*not*	Febuary
accidentally	*not*	accidently
perform	*not*	preform
dangerous	*not*	dangrous

B Exaggerating certain sounds is a useful strategy. For example, when you wish to spell extraordinary, say to yourself:

EXTRA ordinary

describing it more fully: *A library union objected to the hiring of*

C Try to exaggerate the sounds of highlighted letters in the words below.

chocolate	handkerchief	subtle
laboratory	leopard	cupboard
diamond	Wednesday	often
shepherd	mortgage	interesting

Words in History: leopard—This word comes from the ancient Greek word *leopardos*, which meant a "lion panther." *Leon* ("lion") + *pardos* ("panther"). That's why there is a silent e!

✓ More words with misleading pronunciations are found on page 134.

STRATEGY # 6

Spelling patterns

A Link the word you are learning to spell with other words which have a similar spelling pattern.

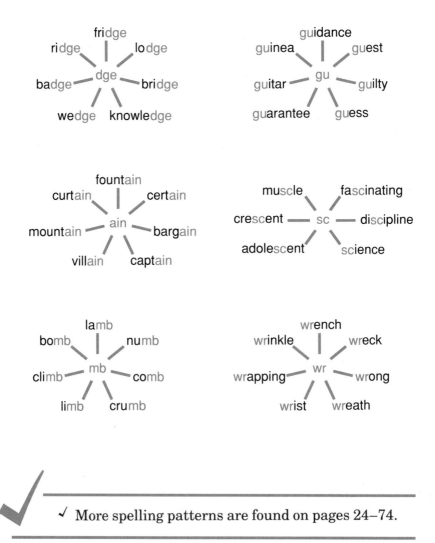

✓ More spelling patterns are found on pages 24–74.

STRATEGY # 7

Looking for the base word

A Long words are often made up of a base word to which prefixes and suffixes have been added. It will be easier to remember the spelling of these words if they are broken down into their meaningful parts.

Looking for the base word.

	Prefix	Base	Suffix
unreasonable	*un–*	reason	*–able*
bicycle	*bi–*	cycle	
refreshment	*re–*	fresh	*–ment*
unacceptable	*un–*	accept	*–able*
irresistible	*ir–*	resist	*–ible*
transportation	*trans–*	port	*–ation*
illogical	*il–*	logic	*–al*
international	*inter–*	nation	*–al*
subcontractor	*sub–*	contract	*–or*
indirectly	*in–*	direct	*–ly*

B Notice that the base word is sometimes changed when a suffix is added.

Base word	Altered form
produce	reproduction
response	irresponsible
scope	microscopic
sense	extrasensory
economy	uneconomical
nature	supernatural
history	prehistoric
mature	immaturity
fortune	unfortunately
migrate	immigration

C Very long words are often used in advertising to make a product appear to have a scientific background.

Made with **POLY**UNSATURATED Fats

✓ You can find more information about base words, prefixes, and suffixes on pages 66–74.
✓ Lists of common words which have prefixes and suffixes are on pages 182–194.

STRATEGY # 8

Using related words as an aid to spelling

A Words which are related in meaning are usually related in spelling. It is often possible to remember difficult letters in a word by reminding yourself of a related word in which the spelling is clear.

B Look at the word pairs below. One word in the pair has a silent letter which, in the related form, is sounded. By thinking of the related word, you will remind yourself of the silent letter in the other.

Base word *silent consonant*	Related word *consonant is sounded*
bomb	bombard
muscle	muscular
sign	signal
design	designation
resign	resignation
condemn	condemnation

C When words have more than one syllable, it is often difficult to hear the vowels clearly in the unstressed syllables. Such vowels are called **schwa vowels**. The dictionary symbol for a schwa vowel is /ə/. The base word, however, often has the same vowel sounded. By referring to the base word, you can often discover the correct spelling of the schwa or unstressed vowel.

1. In the following words, the *schwa* vowel in the related form is clearly sounded in the base word.

Base word	Related word
vowel sounded	*unstressed vowel /ə/*
admire	admiration
compose	composition
propose	proposition
compete	competition
define	definition
repeat	repetition
explain	explanation

D Sometimes the process is reversed. In the following list, the base word has the schwa vowel, while it is sounded in the related form.

Base word	Related word
unstressed vowel /ə/	*vowel sounded*
politics	political
final	finality
comedy	comedian
major	majority
economy	economic
remedy	remedial

✓ More information about *Related words* can be found on page 55.
✓ Lists of *Related words* appear on pages 170–173.

STRATEGY # 9

Systematic word study

A Sometimes all that is necessary to remember the spelling of a word is careful study using some of your five senses.

1. When you need to study a word, use these steps:

Remember to....	
Look at the word, letter by letter, from beginning to end.	✓
Say the word to yourself and listen carefully to the sounds.	✓
Cover the word.	✓
Write the word.	✓
Check the spelling, letter by letter, with the word.	✓

B If you make a mistake in spelling a word, investigate. Did you make a mistake at the beginning of the word? Or in the middle? Or at the end? Was your mistake with a consonant letter? Or a vowel letter? Or both?

C Now try all the steps over again with the corrected word.

Chapter 2
Spelling Patterns

INTRODUCTION

There are many spelling patterns in written English. Good spellers make use of these patterns because they make it possible to avoid memorizing every word separately. For example, when you know the spelling of **right**, it is easier to remember **fight**, **sight**, and **might**. Patterns allow you to chunk the words into categories (*might/fight/sight/right*). You still need to be able to sort out homophones such as **right/write/rite**, **sight/site**, and **might/mite**.

A   You will find spelling patterns in at least four areas of written English:

Sound

1. You will be glad to know that there is a limit to the number of ways certain sounds in English can be spelled. When you are aware of these choices, it makes it easier to spell some words.

a) If a word has the sound /**ou**/, as in **frown**, the /**ou**/ sound is going to be spelled in one of three ways:

- ow (*towel*);
- ou (*bound*);
- ough (*bough*).

b) The task of spelling this sound is now reduced to just three choices, rather than trying out several spellings at random.

Sight

2. Some words form patterns simply because they have unusual features which usually can only be remembered visually.

a) Consider the several words which have a silent **k**, as in **knight, knit, know**. How can you remember the **k** in these words?

Structure

3. There are also many spelling patterns related to adding parts to a base word.

a) You may wish to add /**–ing**/ or /**–ed**/ to a verb such as **hope** (*hope/hoping*).

b) You may decide to make a word plural, **branch/ branches**, or to form a contraction, **I am/I'm**.

c) By knowing the patterns or rules for these changes, you will be much more likely to spell the word correctly.

Meaning

4. Words which are related in meaning are often spelled in a similar way, even if they do not sound the same.

   a) For example, the words **sign, signal**, and **signature**, are spelled in a similar way because they are all based on the word **sign**. A signal and a signature are all types of signs. Therefore, when you need to remember the silent **g** in **sign**, just think of **signal** and **signature** where the **g** is not silent.

   b) Other meaning patterns come about because of the use of prefixes and suffixes, as in **transportation**. Knowing that /**shun**/ must be spelled either /**–sion**/ or /**–tion**/ helps you to avoid spelling this suffix simply as it sounds: *shun*.

B This chapter outlines many spelling patterns. After each pattern is explained, try practising the pattern in ***Chapter 8: Further Investigations***, or look up other examples of this pattern in ***Chapter 7: Word Lists***. You can also use specific spelling strategies given for many of the patterns.

SOUND PATTERNS

Long vowel patterns

A Many long vowels are spelled with a vowel–consonant–silent e. Notice this pattern in the following words:

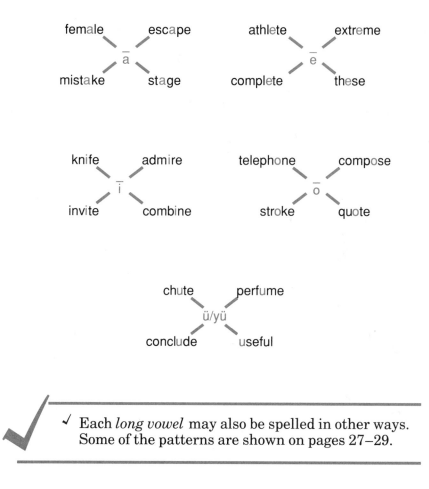

✓ Each *long vowel* may also be spelled in other ways. Some of the patterns are shown on pages 27–29.

long a: /ā/

ai	ay	eigh
painful	crayon	neighbour
sailor	display	sleigh
maintain	maybe	weigh
braid	highway	freight

long e: /ē/

ee	ea	y	ie	i
agree	eagle	gravity	priest	audio
squeeze	release	already	belief	curiosity
wheelbarrow	season	family	shield	delirium
fifteen	weakling	majority	diesel	piano

long i: /ī/

igh	
flight	sigh
thigh	frighten
mighty	nightmare

long o: /ō/

oa	ow	o
boastful	bowling	echo
goalie	yellow	potato
toaster	stowaway	radio
coach	crowbar	bingo

long u: /ü/, /yü/

ui	oo	ew
bruise	cocoon	jewels
suitable	proofread	renew
nuisance	cartoon	curfew
juicy	shooting	chewing

Keep an ongoing list of words in your Personal Dictionary. Consider grouping your words by the word families they represent.

✓ For other words which have the *long vowel patterns* shown above, see pages 27–29.

✓ *Investigations* involving long vowels are found on pages 196–197.

Diphthongs /ou/; /oi/

A The sound /**ou**/ is sometimes spelled **ou** as in **aloud**, or **ow** as in **clown**.

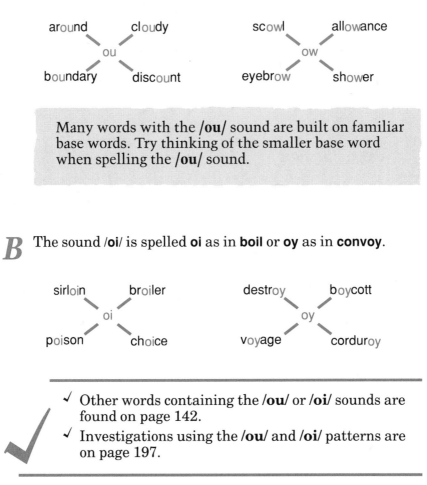

around   cloudy
          ou
boundary   discount

scowl   allowance
          ow
eyebrow   shower

> Many words with the /**ou**/ sound are built on familiar base words. Try thinking of the smaller base word when spelling the /**ou**/ sound.

B The sound /**oi**/ is spelled **oi** as in **boil** or **oy** as in **convoy**.

sirloin   broiler
          oi
poison   choice

destroy   boycott
          oy
voyage   corduroy

✓ Other words containing the /**ou**/ or /**oi**/ sounds are found on page 142.
✓ Investigations using the /**ou**/ and /**oi**/ patterns are on page 197.

R–influenced vowels: /ėr/

A The sound /**ėr**/, as in **birthday** often presents difficulties, because it can be spelled in a number of ways. It is some-times helpful to group words with the /**ėr**/ sound by their spelling patterns.

ur	or	ir
burden	world	circle
disturb	worship	thirsty
furnish	worthy	girdle
urge	worm	confirm

When studying words with the /èr/ pattern, print the letters in a different colour or size.

er	ear
allergy	early
battery	search
observe	heard
reverse	learn

✓ Other words having the /èr/ sound are found on pages 143–145.
✓ *Investigations* for the /èr/ spelling patterns are on page 198.

Variations on consonant spellings /sh/ and /ch/

A The sounds /**sh**/ and /**ch**/ can be spelled in a number of ways. Since there is no way of knowing the correct spelling through the sounds of the words, these words have to be remembered. It often helps to group them by their spelling patterns.

/sh/

ci	sci	ti
ancient	conscious	confidential
suspicion	luscious	initial
gracious	conscience	patient
commercial	fascism	substantial

/sh/

ch	ss
chalet	mission
chaperone	pressure
crotchet	session
mustache	fission

/ch/

t	tch
century	kitchen
situation	butcher
punctual	etching
fortunate	itchy

Use *Strategy # 2* on page 12 to help remember the shape of some of these words. Unusual consonant spellings many times have unusual letter configurations.

SIGHT PATTERNS

EI and IE words

A A simple verse will help you to remember how to spell most words containing ie or ei:

> Put **i** before **e**
> Except after **c**,
> Or when sounded like **ā**
> As in neighbour and weigh

B Notice the following examples of each pattern:

I before e	Except after c	Or when sounded like /ā/
believe	deceive	beige
hygiene	receipt	reign
shield	ceiling	eighth
mischief	perceive	weigh

C There are some exceptions to the patterns described above. Try to remember these:

conscience	height	seize
foreign	leisure	species
forfeit	neither	weird

✓ Other words containing **ei** or **ie** are found on page 147.
✓ *Investigations* related to **ei** or **ie** words are on pages 199–200.

Silent letters

A In some consonant pairs, one of the consonants is **silent**. Such words present special difficulties in spelling since the writer cannot rely on sound for clues.

B Notice the patterns of the silent consonants below. It helps to group words with the same silent letters when you are trying to learn this pattern.

Silent b	Silent g	
mb	*gh*	*gn*
bomb	brought	align
crumb	thorough	assign
plumber	straight	design
tomb	flight	gnash

Silent k	Silent l	
kn	*lm*	*lk*
knack	calm	talkative
knowledge	salmon	yolk
knuckle	palm	folklore
knight	balm	stalk

Silent t	Silent h	Silent w
st	*rh*	*wr*
castle	rhyme	wrestle
hasten	rhythm	wrinkle
moisten		wrist
wrestler		wrestler

Silent u		
ui	*ua*	*ue*
biscuit	guard	guess
disguise	guarantee	guest
guilty	guardian	
building		

C Words with silent consonants may also be remembered by copying the shape of the word using lines or configuration boxes. In this way, the visual clues will help to make up for the lack of sound clues.

align   thumb

knight   yolk

✓ Other words which have *silent consonants* are found on pages 148–150.

✓ *Investigations* related to silent consonants are on page 201.

✓ *Strategy # 2* may be helpful here. It's on page 12.

Unstressed endings

A Many words have **unstressed endings**. It is difficult to hear and decipher the vowel letter (a,e,i,o,u) which spells this vowel sound. Such sounds are called *schwa vowels /ə/.*

B It may help to remember the spelling of unstressed endings by grouping words according to the spelling patterns.

Final /èr/ sounds: er, or, ar

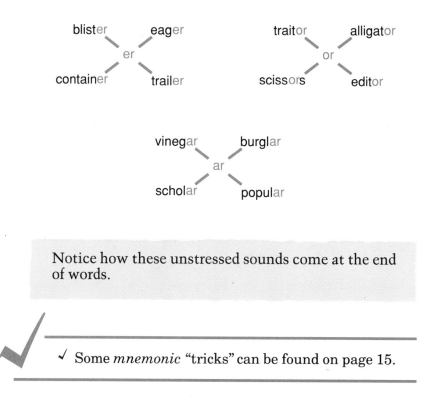

Notice how these unstressed sounds come at the end of words.

✓ Some *mnemonic* "tricks" can be found on page 15.

Final /it/ or /ət/ sounds: it, et, ot, ate

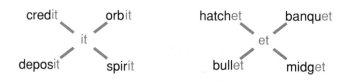

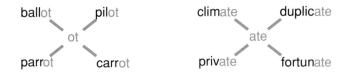

ballot   pilot
ot
parrot   carrot

climate   duplicate
ate
private   fortunate

Final /l/ or /əl/ sounds: le, al, el

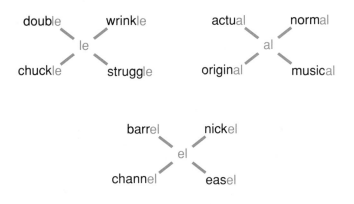

double   wrinkle
le
chuckle   struggle

actual   normal
al
original   musical

barrel   nickel
el
channel   easel

Final /n/ or /ən/ sounds: en, on, in, ain

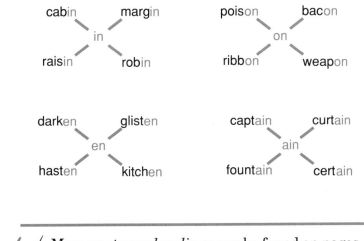

cabin   margin
in
raisin   robin

poison   bacon
on
ribbon   weapon

darken   glisten
en
hasten   kitchen

captain   curtain
ain
fountain   certain

✓ More *unstressed endings* can be found on pages 151–154.
✓ *Investigations* can be found on pages 201–202.

STRUCTURAL PATTERNS

Compound words

A **Compound words** are made up of two or more words which have a logical connection in meaning. In most cases all the letters in the smaller words are used in the compound.

B In the following compounds, the double consonants can be remembered by looking at the smaller words.

> Try thinking of compound words as *two separate words*. This strategy might help you to remember the double consonants.

hitch	+	hiker	=	hitchhiker
night	+	time	=	nighttime
room	+	mate	=	roommate
jack	+	knife	=	jackknife
grand	+	daughter	=	granddaughter
glow	+	worm	=	glowworm
ear	+	ring	=	earring
book	+	keeper	=	bookkeeper
with	+	hold	=	withhold

✓ Other lists of *compound words* are found on pages 154–156.

✓ *Investigations* based on compound words are on page 203.

Contractions

A A contraction is a shortened form of two words. One or more letters are removed and replaced by an apostrophe, as in you're/you are.

B In most cases, you can remember where to place the apostrophe by thinking of the part of the second word which is no longer heard in the contraction. For example:

a) had not/hadn't
- The /o/ sound in **not** is not heard in the contraction **hadn't**.

b) that is/that's
- The /i/ sound in **is** has been lost in the contraction **that's**.

c) you have/you've
- Only the /v/ sound in **have** remains in the contraction.

d) do not/don't
- The /o/ sound in **not** is dropped in the contraction.

e) we would/we'd
- Only the /d/ sound in **would** remains in the contraction.

✓ Other *contractions* are found on page 157.
✓ *Investigations* on contractions are on page 204.

Plurals

A There are a number of patterns for changing nouns from the singular form to **plural**.

1. To form the plural of most nouns add **s**.

Singular	Plural
synonym	synonyms
uniform	uniforms
promise	promises
ski	skis

2. To form the plural of nouns ending with **s**, **sh**, **ch**, and **x** add **es**.

Singular	Plural
s	*–es*
bus	buses
circus	circuses
octopus	octopuses
surplus	surpluses
ss/sh	*–es*
actress	actresses
address	addresses
compass	compasses
eyelash	eyelashes

Singular	Plural
ch	*—es*
beach	beaches
scratch	scratches
sandwich	sandwiches
speech	speeches
x	*—es*
prefix	prefixes
reflex	reflexes
suffix	suffixes

Words in History: Sandwich—Named after the British Earl of Sandwich (1718–92). He wanted something to eat without leaving the gambling table.

3. To form the plural of nouns ending in y:

a) If the **y** is preceded by a *vowel*, as in **turkey**, add **s**.

Singular	Plural
chimney	chimneys
attorney	attorneys
valley	valleys
monkey	monkeys

b) If the **y** is preceded by a *consonant*, as in **allergy**, change the **y** to **i** and add **es**.

Singular	Plural
allergy	allergies
biography	biographies
country	countries
luxury	luxuries

4. To form the plural of nouns ending in **o**, add **s**.

Singular	Plural
banjo	banjos
radio	radios
studio	studios
video	videos

a) Here are some exceptions to the pattern for nouns ending in **o**.

Singular	Plural
domino	dominoes (or dominos)
echo	echoes
embargo	embargoes
hero	heroes
mosquito	mosquitoes (or mosquitos)
potato	potatoes
tomato	tomatoes
torpedo	torpedoes
veto	vetoes
volcano	volcanoes (or volcanos)

What is the pattern for these exceptions?

5. To form the plural of nouns ending with **f** and **fe**, add **s**.

Singular	Plural
belief	beliefs
chief	chiefs
roof	roofs (or rooves)
sheriff	sheriffs
giraffe	giraffes

a) There are a few exceptions to the pattern for words ending in **f** and **fe**. All change to **ves**.

Singular	Plural
calf	calves
elf	elves
half	halves
knife	knives
leaf	leaves
life	lives
loaf	loaves
self	selves
shelf	shelves
thief	thieves
wife	wives
wolf	wolves

✓ For more *plural words* turn to pages 158–161.
✓ *Investigations* start on page 205.

Plurals: special forms

A Irregular forms.

Singular	Plural
child	children
man	men
woman	women

B Plurals of words ending with *–ful*, add **s**.

Singular	Plural
cupful	cupfuls
handful	handfuls
teaspoonful	teaspoonfuls

C Plurals of letters, numbers, and words—add apostrophe (**'**) and **s**.

Singular	Plural
1990	the 1990's
v	three v's
6	five 6's
and	three and's

D Plurals of proper nouns—add **s** or **es**.

Singular	Plural
Hudson	the Hudsons
Michalopoulus	the Michalopouluses
Murphy	the Murphys

E Some nouns keep their Latin plural forms.

Singular	Plural
analysis	analyses
crisis	crises
criterion	criteria
diagnosis	diagnoses
datum	data
hypothesis	hypotheses
medium	media
phenomenon	phenomena

✓ Lists of other *plural nouns* are found on pages 160–161.
✓ *Investigations* dealing with plurals are on pages 205–206.

Possessives

A The **possessive** form of a noun shows ownership. There are several patterns for forming possessives.

1. When a noun is singular, such as **doctor**, add apostrophe (') and **s**.

Singular	Possessive
child	child's
goalie	goalie's
witness	witness's
baby	baby's
referee	referee's

2. When a plural noun already ends in **s**, such as **players**, add just an apostrophe (**'**).

Singular	Plural	Plural possessive
player	players	players'
goalie	goalies	goalies'
baby	babies	babies'
judge	judges	judges'
witness	witnesses	witnesses'

3. For plural nouns, such as **men**, add apostrophe (**'**) and **s**.

Singular	Plural	Plural possessive
man	men	men's
woman	women	women's
child	children	children's

Possessives are easier to remember if you try switching the sentence around. **Referee's whistle: The whistle of the referee.** Notice whether the base word is singular or plural.

✓ Lists of *possessive* forms are found on page 162.
✓ *Investigations* on possessives are on page 206.

Adding endings: Y to I

A There are two patterns which can usually be used for adding suffixes to words ending in a **consonant + y**, as in **satisfy**.

1. Adding suffix beginning with **i** (such as *–ing*):

apply	+	*–ing*	=	applying
classify	+	*–ing*	=	classifying
occupy	+	*–ing*	=	occupying
marry	+	*–ing*	=	marrying

Keep the final **y** when adding a suffix beginning with the letter **i**.

Word quiz: Why did the fly fly? *Because the spider spied her.*

2. Adding suffixes beginning with a letter other than **i**:

apply	+	*–ed*	=	applied
classify	+	*–ed*	=	classified
occupy	+	*–ed*	=	occupied
marry	+	*–ed*	=	married
angry	+	*–ly*	=	angrily
clumsy	+	*–ness*	=	clumsiness
envy	+	*–ous*	=	envious
funny	+	*–est*	=	funniest

Change the **y** to **i** when adding all other suffixes.

3. The pattern in number 2 above is followed when forming plurals of nouns ending in a **consonant + y**.

Singular				Plural
city	+	*–s*	=	cities
enemy	+	*–s*	=	enemies
grocery	+	*–s*	=	groceries
memory	+	*–s*	=	memories

Change the **y** to **i** when adding all other suffixes.

✓ Lists of words related to this pattern are found on page 163.
✓ *Investigations* for adding suffixes to words ending in **consonant + y** are on page 207.

Adding endings: words ending in silent e

A Remember the two patterns below when adding suffixes to words ending in **silent e**, such as **achieve**.

1. Suffixes beginning with a **vowel** or **y**:

approve	approval
encourage	encouraging
propose	proposal
separate	separating
juice	juicy

2. Suffixes beginning with a **consonant**:

absolute	absolutely
arrange	arrangement
peace	peaceful
involve	involvement

- *Drop* the **silent e** when adding a suffix beginning with a vowel or y.
- *Keep* the **silent e** when adding a suffix beginning with a consonant.

Did you know that **e** is the most commonly used letter in the English language?

B Here are some exceptions to the above patterns:

abridge	abridgment (or abridgement)
acknowledge	acknowledgment (or acknowledgement)
argue	argument
awe	awful
courage	courageous
double	doubly
due	duly
horrible	horribly
incredible	incredibly
judge	judgment (or judgement)
notice	noticeable
nine	ninth
outrage	outrageous
possible	possibly
probable	probably
terrible	terribly
true	truly
twelve	twelfth
wide	width
wise	wisdom
whole	wholly

✓ More words with a *silent e ending* start on page 165.
✓ *Further investigations* are on pages 209–210.

Adding endings: doubling before suffixes

A There are a number of patterns to remember when doubling consonants in words with suffixes. This pattern is often the cause of many spelling errors.

Single–syllable words

1. Adding endings to single–syllable words with a single vowel followed by a single consonant, as in **shrug**:

blur	blurred	blurring
knit	knitted	knitting
flip	flipped	flipping
scar	scarred	scarring

Double the final consonant when adding **–ed** or **–ing**.

Two–syllable words

2. The pattern for doubling consonants in two–syllable words depends upon which syllable is stressed.

a) Two–syllable words ending with a single vowel and a single consonant, and the final syllable is stressed, as in **occur** (oc cur′):

acquit	acquitted	acquitting
control	controlled	controlling
propel	propelled	propelling
regret	regretted	regretting

Double the final consonant when adding **–ed** or **–ing**.

b) Two–syllable words ending with a single vowel and a single consonant, and the first syllable is stressed, as in **happen** (hap′pən):

reason	reasoned	reasoning
pilot	piloted	piloting
profit	profited	profiting
pardon	pardoned	pardoning

Do not double the final consonant when adding **–ed** or **–ing**.

B The exceptions to the above patterns in Canadian and British spellings are shown below. Although both spellings are considered acceptable, the *first one* is usually the one most often used.

Base word	*–ed*	*–ing*
label	labelled (labeled)	labelling (labeling)
travel	travelled (traveled)	travelling (traveling)
shovel	shovelled (shoveled)	shovelling (shoveling)
cancel	cancelled (canceled)	cancelling (canceling)
equal	equalled (equaled)	equalling (equaling)
model	modelled (modeled)	modelling (modeling)
shovel	shovelled (shoveled)	shovelling (shoveling)

Notice how all the base words end in **l**.

✓ *Strategies #1 and #2*, on pages 11–13, can be used when learning this pattern.
✓ For a list of words with this pattern, turn to page 167.
✓ *Investigations* are on page 211.

Other doubling patterns

> When a prefix and/or a suffix creates a double conso-
> nant word, think of the *prefix*, *suffix*, and *base word*
> separately.

A   Some words have a double letter where the **prefix** joins the word.

immortal	misspelled
accountant	suggestion
co–operate	surrender
dissolve	unnatural

B   Other words have a double letter where the **suffix** joins the word.

control	controller
electrical	electrically
magical	magically
musical	musically
star	starry

C   In addition to these patterns, the words below also have *double consonants*.

aggressive	commotion	necessary	professional
appreciation	difficult	occasional	sheriff
attitude	errand	occur	squirrel
battalion	essential	opportunity	stubborn
barrel	exaggerate	paraffin	vaccinate
bubbling	hiccup	parallel	vanilla
challenge	missile	penicillin	warrant

✓ Words which have *double letters* can be found on pages 167–169.

✓ *Strategy #2*, on page 12, might help you with this pattern.

Related words

A An important principle you should remember in the spelling system of English is that words which are related in *meaning* are usually related in *spelling*, even if they do not sound the same.

/t/ to /sh/

1. The sound /t/, in the base word, changes to the sound **/sh/**, in the related form, when a suffix is added. But the **t** spelling remains the same.

Base word	Related form
detect	detection
duplicate	duplication
recollect	recollection
exhibit	exhibition
violate	violation

Long vowel to short

2. A long vowel in the base word is changed to a short vowel in the related form, but the spelling of the vowel *remains the same*.

Base word	Related form
athlete	athletic
extreme	extremity
grateful	gratitude
nation	national
severe	severity

Long vowel or short vowel to schwa /ə/

3. In the words below, a short or long vowel in the base form changes to a schwa vowel in a related form. Schwa vowels, usually found in unstressed syllables, create spelling difficulties *because they are not clearly sounded*.

a) It is often possible to recall the correct spelling of a schwa vowel by thinking of a related word in which the vowel is not schwa.

Base word	Related form
admire	admiration
deprive	deprivation
oblige	obligation
compose	composition
install	installation
ecology	ecological
inform	information
specific	specify

Silent consonant to sounded

4. Sometimes a silent consonant in one form of a word is sounded in a related form. It is easier to recall the silent letter if you think of the two forms together.

Base word	Related form
bomb	bombard
column	columnist
muscle	muscular
resign	resignation
condemn	condemnation

Other related patterns

5. Notice the patterns shown below. If you remember these in groups, it is easier to predict the spelling of an unfamiliar word which fits the pattern.

Base word	Related form
ume	*ump*
assume	assumption
consume	consumption
presume	presumption
ceive	*cep*
deceive	deception
perceive	perception
receive	reception

Base word	Related form
nounce	*nunc*
denounce	denunciation
pronounce	pronunciation
vowel + t(e)	*c + suffix*
accurate	accuracy
delicate	delicacy
private	privacy
diplomat	diplomacy
secret	secrecy
ent/ant	*enc/anc*
agent	agency
consistent	consistency
frequent	frequency
president	presidency
vacant	vacancy

✓ A list of more *related words* are on pages 170–173.
✓ *Investigations* can be found on pages 213–214.

MEANING PATTERNS

Homophones

A **Homophones** are words that sound the same but have different meanings and spellings. Because it is not possible to remember the correct spelling of each homophone through its sound, it is important to focus on the meaning and visual form.

1. Try to use memory "tricks" or *mnemonic* devices to sort out homophone pairs. For example:

   a) week/weak
   - I like tea to be weak.

   b) bare/bear
   - I don't dare to go bare!
   - Did you eat the bear meat?

   c) vain/vein
   - The nurse put the needle into the vein.

   c) through/threw
   - We threw out the stew since it was too tough to chew.

2. Another useful strategy for remembering homophones is to look for short forms of the words which may help you to remember the meanings. For example:

   a) Remember **hear** in **heard**.

   b) Remember **four** in **fourth**.

   c) Remember **allow** in **allowed**.

   d) Remember **loud** in **aloud**.

✓ A list of other *homophone* pairs is on pages 173–174.

✓ *Investigations* for homophones are on page 215.

✓ Look for strategies using *mnemonic* devices on page 15.

Borrowed words in English

A Some English words are difficult to spell because they have been **borrowed** from other languages. These languages often have spelling patterns different from those of English.

1. Listed below are some English words borrowed from a variety of languages.

English word	Comes from	Language origin
bagel	*beygel*	Yiddish
banana	*banana*	West African
barbecue	*barbacoa*	Spanish
cafeteria	*cafetero*	Spanish
coleslaw	*koolsla*	Dutch
crystal	*krystallos*	Greek
freckles	*frakel*	Old Norse
judo	*judo*	Japanese
kindergarten	*kinder+garten*	German
knuckle	*kneukel*	Dutch
lilac	*nilak*	Persian
limousine	*Limousin*	French
mattress	*matrah*	Arabic
moose	*moose*	Algonquin
mortgage	*mortgage*	French
nickel	*kupfernickel*	German
nuisance	*nuisance*	French
penguin	*pen gwyn*	Welsh
pretzel	*brezel*	German
raccoon	*arakun*	American Indian
reindeer	*hreindyri*	Old Norse
robot	*robota*	Czech
salad	*salade*	French
shamrock	*seamrog*	Irish
snorkel	*schnorchel*	German

English word	Comes from	Language origin
syrup	*sharab*	Arabic
tornado	*tronada*	Spanish
typhoon	*taai fung*	Chinese
wicker	*viker*	Swedish
yacht	*jacht*	Dutch

✓ Turn to **Spelling strategies** on pages 10–23 for
suggestions on learning difficult to spell words.

Latin words in English

A **Latin**, the language of the ancient Romans, forms the basis
of many English roots. These roots are usually combined
with a prefix, a suffix, or both. By becoming aware of many
Latin roots, prefixes, and suffixes, it will be easier to remember the spelling of many English words.

1. Below is a list of English words borrowed from Latin. How many do you use?

English	Latin	Meaning
alibi	alibi	elsewhere
ambition	ambition	seeking votes
antenna	antenna	feeler of insects
aquarium	aquarium	a watering spot
audience	audientia	audience
benefit	bene	good
bonus	bonum	a good thing
camera	camera	a room
canal	canalis	a water pipe
century	centum	one hundred
circus	circum	around
companion	companio	companion
devout	devotus	devout
duplex	duo + plic	fold
evaporate	evaporare	to evaporate
focus	focus	point toward which lines converge
index	index	a pointer
junior	junior	of lower standing
lantern	lantern	lantern
library	librarium	a library
medicine	medicina	pertaining to a doctor
medium	medium	middle
pedestrian	pedes	foot
percent	per + centum	per hundred
petroleum	petroleum	petroleum
pyramid	pyramis	pyramid
radius	radius	radius of a circle
spectator	spectare	look at
supervision	supervisus	supervision
sponge	spongia	a sponge
territory	territorium	land around a town
virus	virus	poison of a disease
vitamin	vita	life

Latin roots

A A word root, such as **duc**, is a word part which has meaning but cannot stand on its own as a word. In this sense, a word root is different from a base word, such as **invite**. **Base words** are words which can be used as words by themselves.

B The following lists show some Latin roots which are common in English:

1. Pose—from the Latin verb *ponere*, meaning "to put" or "to place":

depose	opposite
disposal	posture
imposter	transpose

2. Fer—from verb *ferre*, meaning "to bring" or "to carry":

confer	offering
differ	preferable
infer	refer
inference	transfer

3. Tract—from verb *trahere*, meaning "to draw":

abstract	distract
contract	extract
detract	retract

✓ For more Latin roots, turn to pages 177–179.

Greek words in English

A The English language was also influenced strongly by the Greeks. Here are some English words which were borrowed from **Greek**.

Since many words which come from the Greek language are long, try breaking such words into syllables.

English	Greek
alphabet	*alpha + beta*
atlas	*Atlas*
automatic	*automaton*
character	*charakter*
cylinder	*kulindros*
democracy	*demokratia*
gymnasium	*gymnasion*
marathon	*Marathon*
orchestra	*orchestra*
phonograph	*phone + graphos*
scheme	*skhema*
tragedy	*tragoidia*
triumph	*triambos*

✓ For more words with *Greek origins*, turn to pages 180–181.

French words in English

A Many **French** words have also been borrowed in English. The sound and spelling patterns of these words have usually remained the same.

English word	Comes from	Meaning
amateur	*amateur*	an amateur
avalanche	*avalanche*	an avalanche
budget	*bougette*	a wallet
bureau	*bureau*	an office
carousel	*carrousel*	a merry–go–round
chauffeur	*chauffeur*	a chauffeur
curfew	*couvre feu*	cover the fire
dandelion	*dent de lion*	tooth of a lion
dungeon	*donjon*	strong cell
limousine	*Limousin*	a town in France
mustache	*moustache*	a mustache
parliament	*parlement*	parliament
revenue	*revenu*	revenue
souvenir	*souvenir*	to remember
tuque	*toque*	knitted stocking

Words in History: curfew—In medieval times, since most buildings were made of wood, there was constant danger of fire. At sunset, a bell was sounded telling people it was time to "cover or put out their fires."

✓ Turn to pages 175–176 for more words that come from the *French language*.
✓ Use some of the suggestions in *Strategy #1*, on pages 11–12, to help you learn these words.

Prefixes: negative prefixes

A A prefix is a word part added to the beginning of a base word. The prefixes **un–**, **non–**, **dis–**, **in–**, **im–**, **il–**, and **ir–**all mean *not*. When one of these prefixes is added to a word, that word takes on the opposite meaning of the base word.

B The words below are examples of these prefixes.

un–	non–
unbearable	nonprofit
unemployment	nonreturnable
unnecessary	nonsense
unfortunately	nonresident

dis–	in–
disappear	inability
dissatisfied	inaccurate
disrespectful	inexpensive
discouraged	inexperienced

The prefix **–im** is a form of **–in**. It also means *not*. It is found before words beginning with **b**, **m**, and **p**. Can you think of any other words?

il–	ir–
illegal	irregular
illegible	irresponsible
illiteracy	irresistible
	irrelevant

C Notice how often *double consonants* occur when a prefix is added to a base word. By separating the prefix and the base word in your mind, it will be easier to remember the double consonant.

✓ Other words with the *same prefixes* are found on pages 182–183.

Prefixes: number

A Some prefixes mean **number** when added to a base word.

uni–: one	*bi–*: two
unicorn	biannual
unison	binomial
unique	bicycle
universal	bicentennial

tri–: three	*semi–*: half; partly
triangle	semicircle
triplicate	semicolon
triplets	semifinal
tripod	semiconscious

triskaidekaphobia means "fear of the number 13."

✓ Other words with *number prefixes* are found on pages 183–184.

Prefixes: opposites

A Certain pairs of prefixes have *opposite* meanings from one another.

- *pre–* means "before," as in **premature**.
- *post–* means "after," as in **postpone**.
- *pro–* means "forward," as in **proceed**.
- *anti–* means "against," as in **antibody**.

Think of the prefix and the base word separately when learning these words.

B Here are some examples.

pre–: before	*post–*: after
prearrange	postoperative
prehistoric	posterity
preview	postwar
prenatal	postdate

pro–: forward	*anti–*: against
proclaim	antifreeze
professional	antisocial
production	antidote
procedure	antiaircraft

✓ More *opposite prefixes* can be found on pages 184–185.

Prefixes: direction

A Three common prefixes show **direction**:
- *trans–* means "across, over, down, or beyond";
- *sub–* means "under or beneath";
- *inter–* means "between or among."

Meaning Patterns

B Look at the words which are directional prefixes. Although many of them are long, they are easier to spell when the prefix is isolated from the base word and suffix.

trans–	sub–	inter–
transcontinental	submarine	intercollegiate
transportation	subscription	intermediate
transfusion	subcommittee	interracial
transformation	subdivision	international

✓ Other words with these *directional prefixes* are on pages 185–186.

Suffixes: noun suffixes

A A **suffix** is a word part added to the end of a base word. Sometimes they affect the spelling of the base words to which they are added.

B These suffixes usually form nouns.

–ment	–ness	–dom
accomplishment	consciousness	boredom
argument	friendliness	kingdom
disappointment	loneliness	martyrdom
requirement	seriousness	wisdom

–ian	–er	–or
comedian	banker	conductor
custodian	farmer	contractor
mathematician	lecturer	director
physician	programmer	spectator
	researcher	

The suffixes –or and –er often mean "one who does."

–ture	–ion	–sion
architecture	communion	admission
departure	opinion	immersion
literature	rebellion	revision
scripture		suspension

–tion	–ation	–ition
affection	cancellation	competition
collection	conversation	definition
duplication	imagination	opposition
edition	registration	recognition

When –ion, –sion, –tion, –ation, and –ition are added to verbs, the words become nouns, as in **admire/admiration**. The spelling of the base word is sometimes affected by the suffix.

✓ For more words with these endings, turn to pages 186–189.

Suffixes: adjective or noun

A The suffixes **–ible** and **–able** are often difficult to remember since they sound very much alike. It may be helpful to know, however, that **–able** is more common than **–ible**. You might also think of tricks or mnemonic devices to remember which suffix to use. For example, " Put the vegetables on the table."

B The suffixes **–ible** and **–able** can mean "capable or worthy of."

–ible	–able
compressible	available
flexible	believable
defensible	correctable
responsible	inflammable

C Trying to figure out the suffixes **–ery**, **–ary**, and **–ory** can be difficult. Sound is also not a reliable clue for remembering these suffixes.

–ery	–ary	–ory
archery	budgetary	advisory
bravery	dictionary	contradictory
greenery	imaginary	explanatory
scenery	missionary	mandatory

Word Quiz: What is more intelligent than a talking parrot? *A spelling bee*.

D The suffixes *–ous* and *–ious* often mean "having or full of."

–ous	–ious
prosperous	felonious
ridiculous	infectious
mischievous	rebellious
continuous	glorious

✓ Lists of other words having these *suffixes* are found on pages 190–191.

Other endings

A Here are some more "suffix–like" patterns which are found often in English. By grouping the words in pattern clusters, it should be easier to remember the spelling of each word.

–ent	–ence	–ant	–ance
different	difference	attendant	attendance
disobedient	disobedience	ignorant	ignorance
excellent	excellence	significant	significance
resident	residence	resistant	resistance

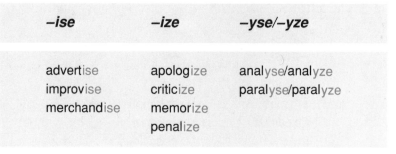

–ise	*–ize*	*–yse/–yze*
advertise	apologize	analyse/analyze
improvise	criticize	paralyse/paralyze
merchandise	memorize	
	penalize	

–ise and *–yze* are very uncommon endings.

✓ For more words with these endings turn to pages 192–194.

Chapter 3
Editing/Proofreading

INTRODUCTION

When you wish to edit a piece of writing, it is important to proofread carefully for spelling errors. Proofreading is a skill which develops with practice. This section of the text will offer you a number of resources to help you become a better proofreader:

- **Ten proofreading strategies:** try the ideas and use the ones that work best for you;

- **A proofreading checklist:** Common spelling problems to guide you in looking for errors in your writing plus reference page numbers for *Spelling Patterns*, *Further Investigations*, and *Word Lists* which deal with that error;

- **Practice proofreading passages:** typical proofreading spelling errors for each of the patterns in Chapter 2, plus reference page numbers for review.

TEN PROOFREADING STRATEGIES

1. Try not to proofread your piece of writing immediately after you have written it. Your attention will still be focussed on meaning rather than the spelling. Wait until the next day.

2. Read your work out loud. You will notice many errors when you read your words to another person.

3. Use a ruler beneath the line you are proofreading to keep track of each line.

4. Proofread from the bottom of the page to the top, or from right to left.

5. Switch papers with a friend. It is often easier to proof-read someone else's work.

6. The first time you proofread a draft, put a mark beside any word you think may be spelled incorrectly. Trust your feelings. If you think a word "doesn't look right," there is a good chance it is misspelled.

7. When you find a word you think is misspelled, try writing it a different way. Does this version "look better"?

8. Be aware of the type of errors you most often make. Go through your work looking for each of these errors in turn. You could also use the *Proofreading Checklist* on the next page.

9. Keep a dictionary beside you as you proofread. Learn to use the *Spelling Chart of Common English Spellings*, similar to the one on page 94, for words whose beginning letters you are unsure of.

10. Record the words you have misspelled in your Personal Dictionary. Consult **Spelling Strategies** on pages 10–23, for help in learning to spell these words.

A PROOFREADER'S CHECKLIST

A Here is a list of the types of spelling errors most frequently made by students. Check your draft for each kind of error during the editing stage of writing.

	Spelling Patterns	Word Lists	Proofreading Passage
1) Long vowel patterns:	27	138	78
long ē: ee, ea, ie	28	139	78
2) R–influenced vowels:			
hurt/dirt/world/her/etc.	30	143	79
3) EI and IE words	33	147	81
4) Silent letters	34	148	82
5) Unstressed endings	36	152	84
6) Homophones:			
reign/rain//rein/etc.	59	173	89
7) Contractions:			
can't/won't/he'll/etc.	39	157	85
8) Possessives:			
my friend's computer/etc.	46	162	87
9) Adding endings:			
Y to I	48	163	88
words ending in silent e	50	165	88
doubling before suffixes	52	167	89

✓ Further help with each type of error can be found under **Spelling Patterns**, **Word Lists**, and **Further Investigations**.

✓ You can also use the *Self-analysis Checklist* on page 8 when looking up a spelling error or pattern.

PROOFREADING PASSAGES

Long vowel patterns

A Here is a suggested strategy for remembering **long vowel patterns**:

1. Keep a list of words which spell the long vowel pattern in the same way.

Long e: /ē/

ee	ea	e–consonant–e
beef	leaf	scene
teeth	dream	concrete
feel	cream	supreme

B Correct any errors involving long vowels in this passage. Only some of the words with long vowels are misspelled.

> We contacted the reel estate agent when we decided to move to this area. Every weekend we toured at least fifteen houses but we could never agree on which one to bye. My mom and dad would thoroughly inspect the inside of the house, while my brother and I were more interested in the nieghbours on the streat. We

*finally had to decide betwean
this house and another one on
Elgin Street. We chose this one,
because the owner offered to
leeve his piano and vidio
recorder as part of the deel.*

FOR SALE

✓ Look up *long vowel patterns*, on page 27.
✓ Word lists with *long vowel patterns* are on pages 138–142.
✓ *Investigations* for long vowel patterns are on pages 196–197.

R–influenced vowels

A Try these suggested strategies.

1. Group words by the way in which the **/ėr/** sound is spelled.

er	ur	or	ir
mercy	purpose	worthless	circle
reserve	urgent	worship	thirty

2. Use *mnemonic* devices or "tricks" to remember how the **/ėr/** sound is spelled:

To remember the u in Saturday, think YOU (U) love Saturday!

3. Use a different colour or larger print to write the letters which spell /èr/:

cIRcuit
pERrsuade

B Correct the misspelled words throughout the letter. All errors involve R–influenced vowels containing the /èr/ sound, as in **first**.

Dear Lisa,

I herd you called me yesterday while I was babysitting. It was my wirst experience ever! I had to help control therteen seven year old girls at a berthday party. The party had a cercus theme, and it was cirtainly a good choice! No one could hear a wird I said over all the noise, and I couldn't pursuade a single person to listen to me. Of course, no one seemed concirned about that – they were too busy birsting balloons and terning up the stereo. Finally, the mother took murcy on me and let me leave a bit erly. What a way to urn a living!

✓ Spelling patterns for *R–influenced* vowels are on pages 30–31.
✓ More words for this pattern are on pages 143–145.
✓ **Further Investigations** can be found on page 198.

EI and IE words

A Suggested Strategies:

- review *EI and IE* words in **Spelling Patterns** on page 33;
- use these rules when doing **Further Investigations**;
- test your knowledge in *proofreading passages*.

B Look at the spelling errors in the newspaper report below. All the errors involve words containing the EI or IE combination. (But keep in mind that not all the EI or IE words are misspelled!)

Arson Suspected

Arson is beleived to be the cause of several brush fires in fields throughout the area last weekend. In a breif news conference, Fire Cheif Louis Argo reviewed the events of the past few days and helped piece together a pattern of fires that seemed to

have been set deliberately. (The police had recieved an anonymous tip.)

Nieghbours in the areas of the fires reported seeing several unidentified suspects setting grass fires just for mischief on Friday and Saturday evenings. Chief Argo said there could have been a feirce blaze in each case, but that relief was provided by the rainy weather. The investigation continues.

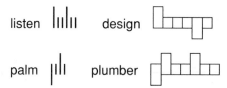

✓ **Spelling Patterns** for *EI and IE* words are on page 33.

✓ **Word Lists** for this pattern are on page 147.

✓ Turn to pages 199–200 for **Further Investigations**.

Silent letters and letters not clearly pronounced

A When thinking of strategies consider these two:

1. Exaggerate the pronunciation of the word to highlight the letters not sounded.

Wed NES day   mus Cle

2. Use configuration to remember the shape of the word.

listen   design

palm   plumber

B Try to fix the passage on the next page. Each contains a number of errors in words which have silent letters or sounds that are not clearly pronounced in everyday speech.

When children lissen to nursry rhymes and fokelore, they offen remember these stories for the rest of their lives. How many of these tales or rymes do you reconize?

- The poor girl who went in disgise to a ball and had to leave quickly at midnight.
- The damsel who had been locked in a cassle tower by an evil wich. She let her long, strait hair and was visited by a prince who climed up her hair to her room.
- The little girl whose lam followed her to school one day.
- The wolf who nocked on the door of innocent animals.
- The emperor who surprized everyone by wearing no close. These intresting tales and others are all found in your libary.

✓ **Spelling Patterns** for *silent letters* are on pages 34–35.
✓ Words with *silent letters* can be found on pages 148–150.
✓ Look up *misleading pronunciations* in **Chapter 6: Spelling Demons** on page 134.
✓ **Further Investigations** are on page 201.

Unstressed endings

A Here are two suggested strategies to help you:

1. Leave a blank for the letter that is hard to remember in the unstressed ending:

   cous__n   nick__l

   a) Focus on the letter as you fill in the blank:
   - write this letter in a different colour;
   - use larger letters;
   - underline it;
   - or use a "highlighting" pen.

2. Keep a list of words in your Personal Dictionary which spell unstressed endings in the same way.

el	al	le
angel	postal	double
camel	rural	needle
parcel	signal	single
tunnel	moral	wrinkle

B In the following passage, many words with unstressed endings are misspelled. Can you correct each of these errors?

Our school recently held an environmentel awareness week. We learned about the need to preserve the delicit balence in nature. Our climite is being altered at a frightining pace by chemicels which poisen the atmosphere. Throughout the world, endangered animels

struggle to survive in their
originel habitats. We listined
to a panle of severel speakers
who said that limets and
controls must be set at both
the locel and nationel levals.
I personelly learned a great
deal from the week and
hope it becomes an annuel
event.

✓ **Spelling Patterns** for *unstressed endings* are on pages 36–37.
✓ **Word Lists** can be found on pages 151–154.
✓ For more practice, turn to **Further Investigations** on pages 201–202.

Contractions

A There are no "quick and easy" strategies for correcting **contractions**.

- Look up the correct pattern.
- Practise using the correct pattern.

B Kevin and Maria are talking. Correct any errors in the spelling of contractions in their dialogue:

Kevin: Has'nt anyone seen Lars
yet? He promised hed be here
with our stage props.
Maria: Shouldnt' we call his

house in case hes still there?
We shouldve started our
rehearsal already.
Kevin: Youd think hed realize
how important this rehearsal
is. Weve got to be ready to
perform two weeks from today.
(DIANA appears, looking relaxed
and rested.)

Diana: Dont worry, I have'nt
forgotten about the props. I just
had trouble getting up this
morning.....Youre looking at
me as though I'd committed
a crime!
Maria: Yeah, right now you're
on the Most Wanted list!

✓ **Spelling Patterns** for *contractions* are on page 39.
✓ Additional words can be found on page 157.
✓ For *Investigations* turn to page 204.

Possessives

A To correct errors using **possessives**, try learning the patterns and carefully proofreading your writing.

B Don't let these errors possess you! How many possessives have been left out?

Last summer my friends and I spent a day at our citys zoo and aquarium. It was fascinating to see the animals reactions to the crowds around their cages. The monkeys antics were especially funny, since they climbed the mesh fence and took peanuts from each visitors hand. The seals and porpoises performed many tricks to win their trainers approval and a reward of fish. Even the tiny fish in the stream running through the zoo swam eagerly near the shore to snap up the childrens offerings of bread crumbs.

✓ **Spelling Patterns** for *possessives* can be found on pages 46–47.
✓ More words are on page 162.
✓ *Investigations* for possessives are on page 206.

Adding Endings

A The same strategies that you used for *contractions* and *possessives* are helpful when learning how to recognize incorrect endings.

- Look up the correct pattern;
- Practise using the correct pattern.

B Correct any errors involving the adding of endings to words in the series of headlines and advertisements following.

Adding endings to words ending in Y:

— WITNESS TESTIFYS HE SAW ACCUSED DESTROYING EVIDENCE

— AUDIENCE JUDGES FUNNYEST COMEDIAN

— EARTHQUAKE VICTIMS FURYOUS WHEN NOTIFYED OF DELAYS WITH RELIEF MONEY

— STUDENTS APPLYING IN RECORD NUMBERS FOR GRANTS SUPPLYED BY GOVERNMENT

Suffixes and silent E

— ARRANGMENTS BEING MADE FOR FAMEOUS SINGER TO PERFORM

— GREAT EXCITMENT OVER PURCHASE OF VALUEABLE DIAMOND

— COUNCIL STILL ARGUEING OVER HOUSING PROPOSAL

— ABSOLUTELY NO MONEY DOWN – BRING THIS ADVERTISEMENT WITH YOU!

Doubling before suffixes

— REBEL FORCES EQUIPED WITH HEAVY ARTILLERY CONTROLING COUNTRYSIDE

— CAR SLAMED INTO TELEPHONE POLE AND FLIPED SEVERAL TIMES

— INVESTORS WHO PROFITTED FROM ILLEGAL LAND DEAL COMMITED TO TRIAL

— HUNDREDS OF SURVIVORS CRAMED INTO MAKESHIFT HOSTEL EQUIPED FOR ONLY FIFTY

✓ **Spelling patterns** for *adding endings: Y to I* can be found on pages 48–49.

✓ Patterns for *words ending in silent e* are on pages 50–51.

✓ Turn to pages 52–53 to find patterns which illustrate *doubling before suffixes*.

✓ **Word Lists** for these three patterns are on pages 163, 165, and 167.

✓ **Further Investigations** are on pages 207–212.

Homophones

A When trying to proofread for **Homophones**, consider these suggested strategies:

1. Use *mnemonic* devices or "tricks" to remember the correct spelling of homophones.

fair: Her hair was fair
fare: I don't care how much the bus fare is.

2. Link the homophone with a word related in meaning: heard/herd

a) Relate heard to the present tense of the verb "to hear."

B Which homophones below are incorrectly used?

I was feeling board last night, so of coarse I turned on the television. The movie of the weak was a sad tail about sum survivors of a plain crash in the Rockies. There were originally over one hundred passengers on bored, but only for survived the crash. They were all in grate pane and new that there only hope for survival lay in finding medical help. One of the survivors

was an experienced hiker, so he lead the group threw the course underbrush in poring reign. One of the men dyed from loss of blood, and the others were becoming very week, two. They had begun to believe their ordeal had been in vein, when suddenly they herd the faint calls of a search party. Before long they were in the safety of a hospital room. In the final seen they through a grate party to celebrate there rescue.

✓ *Homophone* patterns are on page 59.
✓ More *homophone* words are on pages 173–174.
✓ **Further Investigations** can be found on page 215.

Chapter 4
Using the Dictionary and Thesaurus

USING THE DICTIONARY

Introduction

The **dictionary** is an invaluable resource for writers. Most people realize that the spelling and meaning of a word can be found in a dictionary, but many other types of information are also provided. A typical dictionary entry may show:

- the pronunciation of a word;
- which syllables are stressed;
- sample sentences;
- the etymology or origin of a word;
- synonyms and antonyms;
- idioms involving a word;
- parts of speech;
- inflected forms of a word.

The following section briefly describes each feature mentioned above and suggests how the information found in a dictionary can be put to use in the editing phase of writing.

Locating words

Guide words

A If the beginning letters of a word are known, the word may be found through the use of **alphabetical order**. To make the task of locating entry words more efficient, guide words are located at the top of each dictionary page. For example:

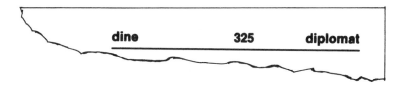

| dine | 325 | diplomat |

1. The guide word **dine** on the left is the first entry on that page. The guide word on the right is the last entry on the page. All other entry words on that page fall between **dine** and **diplomat** in the alphabet.

Common spellings of English sounds

B When the beginning letters of a word are not known, it is more difficult to locate the word in a dictionary. Try these strategies:

1. Make an educated guess about the likely spelling of the word. Try all possible ways of spelling the sound/letter combination.

2. Use the Spelling Chart which is found in most dictionaries. This chart outlines the many ways in which particular sounds in the language can be spelled at the *beginning*, *middle*, or *end* of words.

Common Spellings of English Sounds

	Beginning of Words	Middle of Words	End of Words
r	run, rhyme, wrong	parent, hurry	bear, burr
s	cent, psalm, say science, sword	decent, mason, resuscitate, massive, extra	nice, bogus, miss, lax
sh	chauffeur, schwa she, sure	ocean, machine, special, insurance, conscience, nausea, tension, issue, mission, nation	wish, cache
t	ptomaine, tell thomas	later, latter, debtor	bit, mitt, doubt
th	thin	toothpaste	bath

C Suppose you want to locate the word **science** in the dictionary, but are not sure of the beginning letters. By looking up the sound /s/ on the chart, you would know that this sound can be spelled in five ways when it comes at the beginning of words: **c**, **ps**, **s**, **sc**, and **sw**. By searching the dictionary for each possible beginning letter combination, you would eventually find the correct spelling of **science**.

Pronouncing words

Pronunciation guide and key

A If you know how to spell a word but are not sure of how to say it, the **pronunciation guide** in brackets following each entry word will help you. By understanding the symbols for each sound, you will be able to pronounce any entry in the dictionary.

1. Every dictionary has a pronunciation key which links each symbol with a sound. Look at the pronunciation key below. Notice that each symbol is followed by a key word that tells you the sound.

hat, āge, fär; let, ēqual, tėrm; it, īce
hot, ōpen, ôrder; oil, out; cup, pùt, rüle
əbove, takən, pencəl, lemən, circəs
ch, child; ng, long; sh, ship
th, thin; ŦH, then; zh, measure

Wacky Definition: *cowhide*.

Schwa

B The symbol /ə/ stands for the schwa sound. Notice the schwa symbol in the pronunciation key. As the examples show, any letter can make this sound. The schwa sound is found only in unstressed syllables.

gram·mar (gram′ər) li·cence (lī′səns) post·al (pōs′təl)

Primary and secondary stress

A It is sometimes difficult to know which syllables to stress in an unfamiliar word. The dictionary entry will provide the necessary clues for this task. Each entry word is divided into syllables with a black dot separating each syllable, as in
lim·er·ick.

1. In a word with two or more syllables, at least one of the syllables is said more loudly, or with more stress, than the other. The pronunciation for the word shows which syllable is stressed. An accent mark in **dark type** follows the stressed syllables, as in **lim′it**.

2. Longer words may have two accented syllables. The strongest stress is called **primary stress**, and is shown by an accent mark in dark type. The lighter stress is called **secondary stress**, and is shown in lighter type. For example:
sec·re·tar·y (sek′rə ter′ē)

Investigations

1. Try using the pronunciation key to "decode" these entry words:

a) (nīvz)	**f)** (gok′ē)
b) (kwik)	**g)** (tėr′kwoiz)
c) (griz′ləz)	**h)** (kō ôr′də nā′shən)
d) (fō′tə graf′)	**i)** (ek′ə loj′ə kəl)
e) (sėr′kəl)	

Word meanings
Multiple meanings

A Most entry words have more than one definition. It is important to read all the definitions given in order to understand the word more fully. The first meaning in the dictionary is not necessarily the most common definition, since different dictionaries organize definitions in different ways.

He licks his chops as he chops his chops.

1. Notice the variety of meanings given for the word faint:

> **faint** (fānt) **1** not clear or plain; dim: *faint idea, faint colors. We could see a faint outline of trees through the fog.* **2** weak; exhausted; feeble: *a faint voice.* **3** done feebly or without zest: *a faint attempt.* **4** a condition in which a person is unconscious for a short time, caused by an insufficient flow of blood to the brain: *She fell to the floor in a faint.* **5** lose consciousness temporarily: *He fainted at the sight of his bleeding finger.* **6** ready to faint; about to faint: *I feel faint.* **7** *Archaic.* grow weak; lose courage: *"Ye shall reap, if ye faint not."* 1–3, 6 *adj.*, 4 *n.*, 5, 7 *v.* —**faint′ly,** *adv.* —**faint′ness,** *n.* **feel faint,** feel ready to faint.
> ☞ *Hom.* feint.

Parts of speech

B The variety of meanings for an entry word often reflect different **parts of speech**. Look at the parts of speech for the entry faint:

> 1–3, 6 adj., 5,7 v.

C This abbreviated code translates as follows:

- definitions 1, 2, 3, & 6 are *adjectives*;
- definitions 5 & 7 are *verbs*;
- two other forms of **faint** are **faint′ly**, *adverb* and **faint′ness**, *noun*.

Example sentences

D It is sometimes difficult to understand the meaning of an entry word without seeing it used in the context of a sentence. Notice that many of the meanings given for **faint** are also accompanied by sample sentences:

> **4** a condition in which a person is unconscious for a short time, caused by an insufficient flow of blood to the brain: *She fell to the floor in a faint.*   **5** lose consciousness temporarily: *He fainted at the sight of his bleeding finger.*   **6** ready to faint; about to faint: *I feel faint.*   **7** *Archaic.*   grow weak; lose courage: *"Ye shall reap, if ye faint not."*   1–3,

Homographs

E **Homographs** are words which have the same spelling but different meanings, origins, or pronunciations. Each homograph is given a separate entry in the dictionary. Some examples of homographs are as follows:

- **mail**, meaning "letters," and **mail** meaning "armour";
- **bank**, meaning "the ground bordering a river, lake, etc.," **bank**, meaning "a small container used to save small sums of money at home," and **bank**, meaning "a row of keys on an organ, typewriter, etc.";
- **content**, meaning "what is written in a book or said in a speech," and **content**, meaning "satisfied."

Idioms

F An **idiom** is a phrase or expression whose meaning cannot be understood from the ordinary meanings of its individual words. For example, "I caught a cold" does not mean that you literally *captured* a cold!

1. Some entry words have idiomatic meanings which are different from their simple definitions. These informal expressions are described at the end of an entry.

   a) Look at the sample below taken from the end of the entry for **hit**:

> **hit it off,** *Informal.* agree or get along well with someone: *Tom hit it off well with his new neighbor.*
> **hit the books,** *Informal.* begin to study, especially very hard: *She decided it was time to hit the books.*
> **hit the roof** or **ceiling,** *Informal.* react with a burst of anger: *When their father saw the condition of his car, he hit the roof.*

Etymology

G Many English words are borrowed from other languages. The origin of a word is called its **etymology**. Interesting information regarding the etymology of words is often found at the end of the dictionary entry.

1. The information below concerns the origin of the word **toboggan**:

> **to‑bog‑gan** (tə bog′ən) *Cdn.* **1** a long, light, narrow sleigh with a flat bottom and no runners, and having the front end curved up and back. **2** ride or carry on a toboggan: *We went tobogganing yesterday. The supplies were tobogganed to camp.* **3** decline sharply and rapidly in value: *House prices tobogganed.* **1** *n.,* **2, 3** *v.*
> ☛ *Etym.* Through Cdn. F *tabagane* from an Algonquian word, such as Micmac *tobakun* 'handsled'. 19c.

H This abbreviated statement means that **toboggan** entered our language from the Canadian French word *tabagane*, which was originally borrowed from an Algonquian word; compare the Micmac word *tobakun*, meaning "handsled." It is believed this borrowing happened in the nineteenth century.

Spelling words

Preferred spellings

A Sometimes more than one spelling of a word is correct, although usually one spelling is generally preferred over the others. The form given first in a Canadian dictionary is more common across Canada as a whole. In spite of this, the second form may be more common in certain areas or among certain groups of people.

1. The entries below show two acceptable spellings. The first in each case is the most common across Canada:

theatre	or	theater
airplane	or	aeroplane
cheque	or	check
centre	or	center
program	or	programme

Homophones

A **Homophones** are words which have the same pronunciation but different meanings and spellings. The following sets of words are homophones:

- pair, pear, pare;
- right, write, rite.

B Each member of a set of homophones is given a separate entry in the dictionary. Usually the other homophone forms are shown at the end of the entry, as in the case of the word **flea**.

> **flea** (flē) any of an order of small, wingless, jumping insects that live as parasites on animals, sucking their blood. *n.*
> ☛ *Hom.* **flee.**

Inflected forms

A Writers often know how to spell the base form of a word, but are unsure of the spelling of **inflected** or related forms:

- adding endings, such as *–ed*, *–ing*;
- changing to past tense;
- making the word plural.

B Most inflected forms of a word are shown toward the end of the dictionary entry for that word.

> **oc-cur** (ə kėr′) **1** take place; happen: *Storms often occur in winter.* **2** be found; exist: *"E" occurs in print more than any other letter.* **3** come to mind; suggest itself: *Did it occur to you to close the window?* v., **oc-curred, oc-cur-ring.**

Computer spell checks

A Many word processing programs have a **spelling checker** to help you locate spelling errors in your drafts. When the spell check is used, it searches every word in the draft and tries to match it with a word from its built–in dictionary. If it comes across a word *not* in its dictionary, it will suggest other words which are closely related in spelling or pronunciation. You must then decide whether any of these words are what you actually meant to type in the text of your draft.

B A computer spell check is a very useful device for spotting many spelling or typographical errors, but it does not do all the work for you. You must still decide which of the given choices, if any, fit your text.

1. For example:

I hope I dont cach a cold in this whether.

    a) This sentence has three spelling errors: *dont*; *cach*; *whether*.

2. The spell check might give you the following choices for the first two errors:

dont

A	dent	B	dint	C	dolt	D	don
E	don't	F	dona	G	done	H	dong
I	doni	J	dons	K	donut	L	dost
M	dot	N	ont	O	dante	P	daunt
Q	dawned	R	deigned	S	denied	T	denote
U	denude	V	dined	W	dinette	X	dinned

cach

A	cache	B	cash	C	catch	D	coach
E	cake	F	chace	G	check	H	cheek
I	chic	J	chick	K	chock	L	choice
M	choke	N	chuck	O	cock	P	coke
Q	cook	R	couch	S	czeck	T	kayak
U	ketch	V	kick	W	koch	X	kook

    a) Since only one choice in the twenty–four offerings for each word will be a correct replacement, it is important to examine the list carefully.

3. The third misspelled word in the example sentence, *whether*, is not discovered by the spell check as an error. "Whether" is a homophone for the correct word, *weather*.

> Most spell checks are not able to detect homophone errors.

C A spell check may also fail to discover spelling errors other than homophones.

1. Since a word processing program can only match the words in your text with the words it has in its dictionary, it may be unable to find errors in unusual names, places, or special terms such as those used in a specific subject area.

    a) When the spell check spots a word in your text which is not in its dictionary, it may say "Not Found." You should check these words in your dictionary. If it is a real word, most spell checkers will allow you to add the word to the program's dictionary.

> Remember, while a spell check program on a computer is a valuable tool, it should always be used along with a standard dictionary. A dictionary is the *best resource for spelling a word*.

USING THE THESAURUS

Introduction

A A **thesaurus** suggests *synonyms*, and sometimes *antonyms*, for commonly used words. It is organized much like a dictionary—in alphabetical order.

Sometimes it is tempting to use the longest or most complex word offered by a thesaurus. However, the words you select must be suited to your audience and your purpose for writing.

Imagine, for example, that you re—wrote the nursery rhyme, "Jack and Jill" so that simple words were replaced by more complex ones:

Jack and Jill ascended the moraine
To acquire a container of aqua.
Jack plummeted earthward,
And fractured his cranium,
And Jill arrived at a later date, also plummeting down the moraine.

Which version of the nursery rhyme, the original or the one above, would be most suitable for an audience of young children?

Getting started

A The word *thesaurus* comes from the Greek word, meaning "treasure." This resource is a storehouse of information concerning words. It is a reference tool which all writers should make use of frequently.

1. While dictionaries begin with a specific word and define its meanings, a thesaurus begins with meaning and explores all the words related to that meaning.

B When a writer wishes to express an idea, but is unable to think of the exact words to express the thoughts properly, a thesaurus will be of great help.

1. For example, if the writer is trying to describe a character who is very smart, by looking up the word **smart** in the thesaurus, the following choices are given:

> **smart** *v.* sting, hurt, pain, pierce, prickle, prick, ache, burn, bite, nip. —*adj.* **1** quick, clever, keen, sharp, shrewd, quick-witted, heads-up (*Slang*), alert, intelligent, bright, adroit, adept, canny, prudent, wise, sensible, brainy. **2** harsh, severe, stinging, painful, sharp, keen, pricking. **3** brisk, lively, spry, nimble, vigorous, energetic, active, spirited. **4** fashionable, chic, spruce, trim, dapper, stylish, trig, natty. —*n.* sting, pang, prick, twinge, pain, anguish, affliction, vexation, distress, wound, hurt, affront, insult.
> **ant.** *v.* soothe, relieve, ease, palliate, comfort. *adj.* **1** stupid, dull, slow, obtuse, simple-minded. **2** mild, gentle, soft, bland, moderate. **3** slow, weak, awkward, halt, handicapped. **4** unkempt, shabby, frowzy, dowdy, untidy. *n.* balm, comfort, anodyne, solace, easement, salve.

2. A thesaurus can be consulted at various stages of the writing process.

Pre–writing

A When you are thinking of ways to approach a topic, it often helps to see what categories are included under that topic in the thesaurus. A useful resource for exploring topics is entitled ***Words to Use****. This thesaurus displays words relating to a topic. Such a display can be helpful for organizing a piece of writing. If, for example, you want to write a report on insects, the following ideas are given:

*Published by Gage Educational Publishing Company (1980).

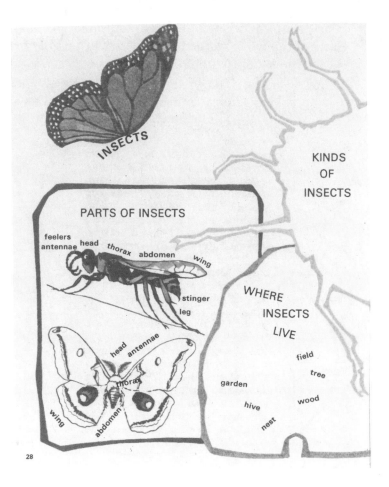

INSECTS

KINDS
OF
INSECTS

PARTS OF INSECTS

feelers
antennae head thorax abdomen wing

stinger
leg

head antennae

thorax

wing abdomen

WHERE
INSECTS
LIVE

field

tree

garden

hive wood

nest

28

Editing

A As you are polishing your writing, you may notice that you have used the same words over and over again. Some tired words and expressions may include **said, glad, walked, sad, like**. By consulting a thesaurus, many other word choices are available to you.

1. For example, the over–used phrase "She said," could be replaced with any of the following:

- She...replied, uttered, commented, suggested, advised, warned, urged, observed.

B It is important to realize, when using a thesaurus, that not *every* word suggested will match your needs. A dictionary should be consulted for the exact meaning of any words of which you are not sure.

1. For example, a thesaurus may give the following choices for the word **anger**:
   - resentment, displeasure, animosity, wrath, indignation, bitterness, exasperation, acrimony.

> *Don't* select words because they look long and complicated.

2. However, each of these words has a slightly different meaning. Each reflects varying degrees of anger.
   a) **Displeasure** expresses a much milder degree of anger than **exasperation**.
3. A dictionary will help you to see the differences among the words offered by the thesaurus.

C It is also important to know how a new word suggested by a thesaurus is used in a sentence. The example sentences in a dictionary entry will often give you this information. For example, it is correct to say, **"I am angry with you,"** but not **"I am resentful with you."** Instead, you should say **"I *feel* resentful *toward* you."**

D Both the dictionary and thesaurus should be standard references which you can consult as a writer, a reader, and a speaker. They are valuable tools in helping you communicate your thoughts and feelings in an accurate and effective way.

Chapter 5
Language Alive

INTRODUCTION

Writers, cartoonists, and politicians share a common skill—
they realize that a single word or phrase can have enormous
impact. This chapter explores the many ways in which
words can be used to create a powerful message. You will see
that writers have many tools for painting a vivid picture in
the reader's mind and for persuading the audience to accept
their point of view.

The English language is very much alive, with some
words dropping out and new terms being created daily. This
chapter looks at how new words are formed in our language.
How did modern terms such as *radar*, *telethon*, *stereo* come
into being? Why do slang expressions change from one year
to the next?

Above all, this chapter shows that observing and playing
with language can be fun! Recording humorous licence
plates, developing riddles, writing "catchy" ads, or creating
effective poetic images—through each of these experiences
you will learn that playing with words is one of the most
effective tools a writer can possess.

INITIALS AND ACRONYMS

A Many names of organizations and familiar word groups are known by their **initials**.

B **Acronyms** are words formed from the first letters or syllables of a series of words. Like initials, they usually refer to organizations, businesses, scientific devices, and so forth.

C The following is a list of some well–known initials and acronyms:

Letters	What they stand for
ac	alternating current (also: AC., A.C.)
a.k.a.	also known as
AM	Amplitude Modification (also: A.M.)
a.m.	ante meridiem—before noon (also: A.M.)
ASAP	As Soon As Possible
AV	Audio Visual
AWOL	Absent WithOut Leave (also: a.w.o.l.)
BLT	Bacon, Lettuce, and Tomato (sandwich)
CBC	Canadian Broadcasting Corporation
C.O.D.	Cash On Delivery (also: c.o.d.)
dc	direct current (also: DC, D.C.)
DOA	Dead On Arrival
GNP	Gross National Product
IOU	I Owe yoU (also: I.O.U.)
IQ	Intelligence Quotient (also: I.Q.)
MYOB	Mind Your Own Business
NSF	Not Sufficient Funds (also: nsf)
p.m.	post meridiem—"after noon" (also: P.M.)
P.O.	Post Office
P.O.W.	Prisoner Of War (also: POW)

Letters	What they stand for
RSVP	Repondez S'il Vous Plait—"please reply"
RCMP	Royal Canadian Mounted Police (also: R.C.M.P.)
SCUBA	Self-Contained Underwater Breathing Apparatus
SIN	Social Insurance Number
SPCA	Society for the Prevention of Cruelty to Animals (also: S.P.C.A.)
STOL	Short TakeOff and Landing
SWAK	Sealed With A Kiss
SWAT	Special Weapons Action Team
TLC	Tender Loving Care
WHO	World Health Organization

Investigations

1. What do the following initials and acronyms stand for? You may need to consult a dictionary for help.

NATO	RV	DEWLINE	R.I.P.
NASA	RADAR	CB	B.A.
COD	DJ	IOU	GP
VIP	SOS	UFO	

2. What acronyms can be made from the following phrases?

   a) ACQUIRED IMMUNE DEFICIENCY SYNDROME

   b) CO–OPERATIVE FOR AMERICAN RELIEF EVERY-WHERE

c) GROUP AGAINST SMOKING IN PUBLIC

d) ORGANIZATION OF PETROLEUM EXPORTING COUNTRIES

e) LIGHT AMPLIFICATION BY STIMULATED EMISSION OF RADIATION

f) SOUND NAVIGATION RANGING

g) UNITED NATIONS INTERNATIONAL CHILDREN'S EDUCATION FUND

3. Can you make up an acronym for a new organization? It could be humorous or serious:

Students Against More Exams: SAME

BLENDED WORDS

A **Blends** are words formed by combining parts of other words. For example, **smog** is a blend of **smoke** and **fog**.

B Here are some blends and the words they come from:

splatter	=	splash	+ spatter
telethon	=	television	+ marathon
flare	=	flame	+ glare
glimmer	=	gleam	+ shimmer
twirl	=	twist	+ whirl
clash	=	clap	+ crash
paratroops	=	parachute	+ troops
splotch	=	spot	+ blotch
motorcade	=	motor	+ cavalcade
flurry	=	fluster	+ hurry

Investigations

1. What words were used to form the following blends? You may need to consult a dictionary for help.

a) brunch   = _____ + _____

b) motel   = _____ + _____

c) smash   = _____ + _____

d) telecast   = _____ + _____

e) cafetorium = _____ + _____

2. The word **cheeseburger** is a blend of the words **cheese** and **hamburger**. The names of many brand name foods are created by blending known foods. How many can you think of?

3. Try creating some "new" food products by blending the names of foods you already enjoy.

LOBSTERWICH!
YUMMY!

CLIPPED WORDS

A Which of the sentences below sounds most natural in every-day speech?

> I was reading the classified advertisements in the news-paper yesterday. There were advertisements for a used refrigerator, a trail bicycle, a gasoline barbecue, and, for music fanatics, a portable microphone and a saxophone.

Or:

> I was reading the classified ads in the paper yesterday. There were ads for a used fridge, a trail bike, a gas barbe-cue, and, for music fans, a portable mike and a sax.

B Many new words are formed by shortening or clipping exist-ing forms.

Investigations

1. Here are some common examples of clipped words:

Clipped words	Long form
copter	helicopter
dorm	dormitory
flu	influenza
memo	memorandum
mums	chrysanthemums
prof	professor
stereo	stereophonic
sub	submarine
van	caravan
vet	veterinarian

2. You probably use the following clipped words at school. What words do they come from?

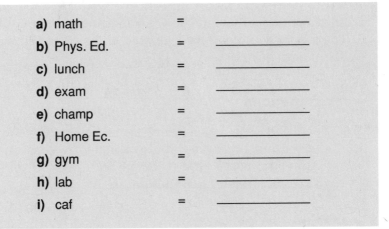

a) math   =   _____

b) Phys. Ed.   =   _____

c) lunch   =   _____

d) exam   =   _____

e) champ   =   _____

f) Home Ec.   =   _____

g) gym   =   _____

h) lab   =   _____

i) caf   =   _____

3. Can you add to the list of clipped words?

ABBREVIATIONS

A **Abbreviations** can be used by a writer to condense or shorten long phrases or terms into more manageable units. Taking notes, writing technical reports, jotting down recipes, or preparing early drafts of a piece of writing—all can use abbreviations.

B Notice the use of abbreviations in the draft of a memo below:

MEMO (draft)

To: All swim coaches
From: Aquatic Dir.
Re: Pool closing

The Rec. Dept. has informed me that the pool will be closed from 10:00 A.M. to 3:00 P.M. on Tues., Jan. 25 This change will affect both Jr. & Sr. classes. Closings will cont. wkly. until mid Feb. while the Maint. Dept. repairs plumbing, repaints the deck, services safety equip. etc. in preparation for the Natl. Meet in Apr.

Please bring these changes to the attn. of your swimmers.

C While abbreviations can be used by a writer to make communication more efficient, they can also make it more difficult. The reader could become confused or distracted if too many abbreviations are used.

Investigations

1. Read the two sets of directions below. **Version 1** is shorter, but has many abbreviations. In **Version 2**, the abbreviations are kept to a minimum. Which version do you think is easier to understand?

Version 1

Follow Hwy. 15 'til jctn. 15 & 34. Turn rt. & go approx. 10 km to Essex Sd. Rd. You'll see lg. constr., site on NW cr. Turn rt. & cont. for 6 km 'til you come to Midland Blvd. The hosp. is on the SE cr.

Version 2

Follow Highway 15 until the junction of 15 and 34. Turn right and go approximately 10 kilometres to Essex Sideroad. You'll see a large construction site on the Northwest corner. Turn right and continue for 6 kilometres until you come to Midland Boulevard. The hospital is on the Southeast corner.

2. In classified ads (*advertisements*), abbreviations are handy when describing an item in the least amount of space. Try to decode the following ads, then rewrite them without abbreviations.

   a) Antique walnut DR suite, 8 pc., exc. cond., $950.
   b) Mates bed w/mattr., match. dresser & desk, $300.
   c) Reg'd. 1 1/2 yr. fem. Border Collie, $200.
   d) Ford Tempo, exc. cond., cert., white ext./red int, PS, air, 4 spkr + deck.

3. Write abbreviations for the following words.

amount	_____	limited	_____	teaspoonful	_____
continued	_____	meeting	_____	weekly	_____
for example	_____	national	_____	weight	_____

JARGON

A Many professions, sports, or hobbies have specialized languages, known as jargon. **Jargon** is usually understood only by people familiar with the specialized area.

B Jargon can add realism to a piece of writing—as long as the reader understands the terms. Readers unfamiliar with the topic, however, may become confused or lose interest.

Investigations

1. Which sport is associated with each set of jargon below?

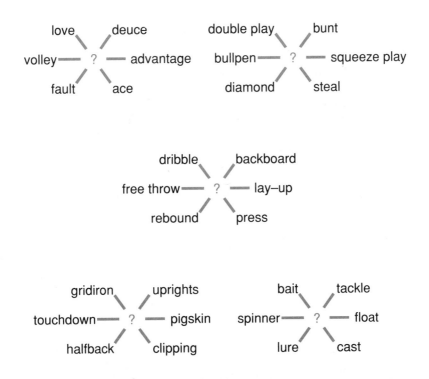

2. The field of computers is adding new jargon to our language every day. Try to explain the terms below to someone who is unfamiliar with computers.

chip boot bug hardware mouse

3. Make up a list of jargon used by people in a particular profession or trade. Use your list to write a brief paragraph which uses several of the terms on your list. Then rewrite the paragraph for a reader who is unfamiliar with the area.

a) Suggested Topics: hairdressers, electricians, actors and actresses, radio/television workers, airline pilots, musicians, fashion designers, auto mechanics.

ONOMATOPOEIA

A **Onomatopoeic** words try to imitate the sound of the object or action they represent.

B Young children often relate onomatopoeic words with particular animals.

C Cartoonists love to use onomatopoeic words to show action in comics.

D Effective writing relies on the use of colourful verbs to express the sounds of an action. Compare the tired verbs with the onomatopoeic verbs below.

Tired	Onomatopoeic
pound	thump, smash, smack
move	clomp, creak, rustle
trip	whack, clatter, flop
dive	splash, plunge
call	squeal, squeak
yell	roar, beep
break	crunch, grind, rip
drink	slurp, chug
eat	chomp, munch
ring	clang, buzz

Investigations

1. a) Write a short paragraph using all of the *tired* verbs on page 119.

b) Now try rewriting your paragraph, substituting onomatopoeic verbs such as the ones above.

c) Which paragraph do you like best? Which is more interesting to read?

A thesaurus is an excellent resource for finding *onomatopoeic* words.

SIMILES

A A simile is a figure of speech which uses the words **like** or **as** to compare two unlike objects. For example, comparing someone to a mule, a person could be described as:

- being as *stubborn* as a *mule*,
- acting like a *stubborn mule*.

Investigations

1. Many similes involve comparisons with animals. Try to complete the similes below with a matching animal name.

a) Proud as a   ————————

b) Slippery as an   ————————

c) Mad as a   ————————

d) Happy as a   ————————

e) Sly as a   ————————

f) Playful as a   ————————

2. Writers can use similes to create vivid images. Complete each simile below in any way you wish. Then compare your similes with those of a partner.

a) The animal crawled along the ground like _____.

b) You are as brave as _____.

c) The surprise party made me feel like _____.

d) Studying for exams is as much fun as _____.

3. As you probably noticed in your responses above, a simile can be created to give a range of impressions, from strongly negative to highly positive. For example, the simile *as funny as a toothache* is intended to mean quite a different message than *as funny as a comedian*.

a) Write at least four similes beginning with the statement, "The rock star looked like _____." Rank them from very negative to very positive.

4. Some similes become **clichés**, expressions which have been used too often. Can you think up new similes for these clichés?

a) as sharp as a tack

b) as white as snow

c) as clean as a whistle

d) as happy as a lark

METAPHORS

A **Metaphors** are similar to similes, since they compare two unlike things. Metaphors, however, do not use the words **like** or **as**. The comparison is not made directly. Metaphors can be used by writers to create powerful descriptive images.

B Notice in the metaphors below that the writer does not expect us to take the comparisons literally. These metaphors, however, still help to visualize the writer's images.

- As I struggled in the quicksand, the mud grew giant tentacles, dragging me beneath the surface.
- The child's pleading gaze became a ghostly presence which haunted me for years to come.
- The pitcher unleashed a fireball—in a split second it lay smouldering in the catcher's mitt.

Investigations

1. **a)** Think of metaphors which could be used to describe the following situations:
   - molten lava spewing out of a volcano;
   - a school bus on the last day of school;
   - a runner at the end of a marathon race;
   - an old car sitting in a used car lot.

   b) Compare your metaphors with those of a partner. How does the choice of metaphors affect the reader's impression of the subject?

2. It has been said that a poem is a "picture painted with words." This metaphor expresses the fact that effective poems create vivid images or pictures in the reader's mind.

   a) Metaphors form the basis of many poems. Work with a partner on developing a series of metaphors or similes based on one of the situations in **1.a)**, above, or on a scene of your own choosing. Arrange the images in the form of a poem.

IDIOMS

A **Idioms** are expressions which are commonly used by speakers and writers. What makes these expressions unique is that their *literal* meaning is very different from their *actual* meaning. For example, it is customary to say to an actor before a performance, "Break a leg!" The purpose of this idiom is to wish the performer "Good luck!" — quite a different interpretation than the literal meaning of the expression!

Investigations

1. Idiomatic expressions can be confusing to individuals who are learning English. How would you explain the following idioms to a friend new to English?

   a) We're really in hot water this time!

   b) That's the way the cookie crumbles!

   c) I'm afraid I can't carry a tune.

   d) Are you feeling blue today?

   e) Every cloud has a silver lining.

2. Sketch a picture or cartoon based on the literal interpretation of an idiom. An example is given below.

3. Many topics have idiomatic expressions of their own. Add other idioms to these categories if you can.

Sports

a) She really went to bat for me.

b) I'm behind the eight ball.

c) We're in the home stretch.

d) He's out in left field.

e) Just roll with the punches.

Animals

f) What a rat race!

g) He's in the doghouse now!

h) You really stirred up a hornet's nest.

i) It's a dog's life.

j) She let the cat out of the bag.

4. Some idioms are based on common words. Explain the differences in meaning in the following idioms based on the verb **hit**:

a) hit the road;

b) hit the ceiling;

c) hit the sack;

d) hit the books;

e) hit the nail on the head.

EUPHEMISMS

A **Euphemisms** are words or expressions which are substituted in order to make an idea less blunt or direct. For example, instead of saying, "You're fired," an employer might substitute the euphemism, "Your position has been terminated."

Investigations

1. Teachers might use euphemisms when reporting a student's progress to parents. Match the euphemisms with the blunt statements on the right.

Euphemisms

your son/daughter...   *blunt statements*

1) has difficulty distinguishing between truth and fiction.

a) fights.

2) needs to gain greater control of aggressive tendencies.

b) steals.

3) should show greater respect for the property rights of others.

c) fools around.

4) has a less than desirable level of motivation.

d) is lazy.

5) should show greater respect when addressing teachers.

e) lies.

6) has been known to borrow answers and assignments from others without their permission.

f) is rude.

7) needs to place less emphasis on socializing while in class.

g) is truant.

8) has difficulty attending school regularly.

h) cheats.

2. Sometimes jobs are given special titles in order to make them seem more glamorous or to give them higher status. Read the euphemisms below and supply the more common job title that goes with each.

a) beautician

b) professional educator

c) landscape technician

d) sales representative for previously owned vehicles

e) sanitary engineer

f) custodian

g) director of human resources

3. A writer's decision to use euphemisms, or more direct terms, is sometimes based on the purpose for the piece of writing. Euphemisms are often used when the writer wants to distort the truth or soften its impact.

a) Imagine a situation in which a giant oil tanker has run aground off the shores of British Columbia. The following facts are known:

- millions of barrels of crude oil are leaking from the vessel;
- huge oil slicks are already visible from the air;
- the fishing industry will be severely damaged for the next few years;
- it is almost certain that millions of fish, birds, and other ocean creatures will die due to the sticky oil;
- the accident occurred because of a navigational error on the part of the ship's captain.

b) You are a public relations officer hired by the ship's owners to soften the bad publicity surrounding the accident. How would you explain to reporters the above facts *without putting the oil company in a very bad light?*

CONNOTATION AND DENOTATION

A The denotation of a word is its dictionary definition. Many words, however, suggest feelings or ideas beyond the literal definition. Such meanings are called **connotations**.

1. The denotation of the word **school** is "a place for teaching and learning." This word, however, carries many connotations beyond the simple definition. Depending on a person's experiences with school, it may bring to mind "friends, good times, success," or possibly "fear, boredom, or a sense of failure."

B Writers must be sensitive to the connotative as well as the literal power of words. Two words may have very similar literal definitions, but quite different connotations. Someone who is underweight, for example, could be described as "slim or skinny." The word **slim** tends to have positive connotations, whereas **skinny** gives a negative impression.

Investigations

1. Substitute a word with a negative connotation for the underlined word in each sentence below:

   a) We spent a quiet evening watching reruns on television.

   b) My cousin is very thrifty with her money.

   c) I decided to give up chocolate bars because I was becoming too plump.

   d) The practical joke was quite amusing.

   e) Last night I babysat some children who were very naughty.

   f) The substitute teacher tried to be strict with the class.

2. Journalists are often able to use the connotative power of words to present a particular viewpoint. Notice the sets of headlines below. In each case, the first headline reveals a positive bias while the second is negative.

- **Cougars fight to the bitter end**
  Cougars give up in final minute of play

- **Dump site approved after careful study**
  Dump site dumped on worried residents
- **Judge shows compassion in sentencing**
  Judge lets criminal off the hook

> **Misleading Names:** *Soda water* has no soda. *Buttermilk* has no butter. *Rice paper* is made from wood pulp, not rice!

a) Write two headlines for each of the following situations. Present a *positive* bias in one version and a *negative* viewpoint in the other.

- Local politician is re–elected to office

- The school board votes to ban all smoking on school property
- A local theatre company stages a new play, and you are reviewing it on opening night

b) Can you write some headlines of your own based on school or community incidents?

3. The real estate section of a newspaper will have many examples of effective use of connotations. These advertisements are not meant simply to sell you a house; they are often designed to appeal to your *emotional* needs as well. In many cases, a negative feature of a house is presented as an asset through the careful use of descriptive words.

   a) Match the positive descriptions with the real problems.

Connotation	Real problem
1. If you want affordability, this is it!	a) very small rooms
2. Large rooms plus old world charm.	b) couldn't dare ask much for this place!
3. Cute and cottagey.	c) owners never repaired a thing! A real wreck!
4. Blends beautifully with million dollar homes on street.	d) huge old home; no modern features
5. In original condition—ready to renovate.	e) looks cheap compared with rest of neighbourhood

Chapter 6
Spelling Demons

INTRODUCTION

These **Spelling Demons** are words which usually give
writers the most trouble when they are proofreading and
editing their words. You might want to look them over. Are
there any that give you trouble? Why not include your
demons in your Personal Dictionary. Use the suggestions
given in *Chapter 7: Word Lists*.

THE 200 MOST COMMONLY MISSPELLED WORDS

about	came	fell
accident	can't	few
actually	catch	field
afraid	caught*	finally
again*	certainly	finished
all	chases	fired
almost	children	first
always	climbed	flowers
and	come	for
animals	coming	found
another*	could	funny
are	couldn't	friend*
around	cousins	girls
away	decided	going
awhile	didn't*	government
back	different	happened
bear	doctor	happily
beautiful*	does	having
because*	doesn't	heard*
been	dollars	here
before	don't	him
began	engine	his
behind	equipment	hole
believe	especially	home
better	ever	horses
bird	every	hospital
birthday	everybody	house
brought	everyday	I'm
built	everything	Indians
buys	exciting	into*
bye	family	its

it's*	piece	take
just	place	than
knew	pollution	that's*
know*	practising	the
let's*	pretty	their*
like	probably	them
lived	quiet	then
looked	quite	there*
met	really	there's
middle	receive	they*
might	responsible	they're
minute	right	things
months	said*	thought
mountains	saw	threw
myself	scared	throw
names	school	to
necessary	screamed	too
neighbour	second	tried
next	shoot	turned
no	shot	two
nothing	situation	until
now	slept	upon*
o'clock	so	very
off*	society	wanted
once	some	wasn't
one	something*	went*
opportunity	sometimes	we're
others	spotted	were*
our*	started	weren't
out	stepped	what's
outside	stopped	when*
parents	strange	where*
parliament	summer	without
people	surely	wouldn't
picked	surprise	writing
pictures	swimming	

*These words are the *twenty-five* most commonly misspelled words.

UNUSUAL SPELLINGS

acreage	cougar	mortgage
anxious	counterfeit	ogre
beige	drawer	pageant
biscuit	feud	questionnaire
boulder	furlough	sleigh
business	guarantee	subtle
canoe	hosiery	succumb
clothes	lawyer	tortoise
cocoa	lieutenant	vehicle
conquer	massacre	

Wacky Definitions: **before**—*What 3 will do if 1 more is added.*

MISLEADING PRONUNCIATIONS

accessories	environment	nuclear
accidentally	escape	numeral
activities	exception	opera
adjective	factory	particularly
adjust	favourite	perform
advertise	formerly	postpone
aluminum	general	probably
arctic	generous	pronunciation
arthritis	governor	pumpkin
athletic	grocery	quantity
average	history	raspberry
battery	interesting	realize
boundary	introduce	recognize
bravery	laboratory	restaurant
budget	length	sandwich
camera	library	secretary
century	lightning	similarity
chimney	literature	similarly
chocolate	maintenance	sophomore
corduroy	memory	strength
dangerous	mineral	subtract
depth	miniature	supposed
diamond	mischievous	surprised
district	natural	temperament
empty	naturally	violet

CONFUSING WORD PAIRS

accept	except
adapt	adopt
advice	advise
affect	effect
alley	ally
altar	alter
angels	angles
bath	bathe
breath	breathe
choose	chose
council	counsel
county	country
custom	costume
dairy	diary
desert	dessert
device	devise
empire	umpire
lose	loose
personal	personnel
preceding	proceeding
recipe	receipt
trail	trial
weather	whether

Chapter 7
Word Lists

INTRODUCTION

Your Personal Dictionary

The words found in this chapter are not intended to be
memorized. They are simply further examples of the spelling patterns described in Chapter 2.

Here are some reasons, however, why you may wish to
add some of these words to your Personal Dictionary.

- The words are grouped by patterns. If you are having
  difficulty with a pattern, such as *contractions* or
  homophones, it is useful to keep your own ongoing list.
- Some of the lists are based on commonly misspelled
  words. Many of these words are ones you use in your
  everyday writing.
- Many of the words reflect the vocabulary of adults. By
  adding some of them to your own list, you will be able to
  increase the range and quality of the vocabulary you use
  in your writing.

There are several other sources of words for your Personal
Dictionary:

- errors you frequently make in the draft forms of your
  writing;

- words you wish to learn from various school subjects;
- words currently being used in the media;
- interesting words you encounter in reading.

Consider these suggestions for making effective use of your Personal Dictionary.

1. Update your list on a regular basis. Add new words and delete those that you are now confident of spelling.

2. Be certain that the words are correctly spelled when adding them to your list.

3. Do not try to study every word in your list at once. Select a manageable number of words.

4. Have a partner dictate the words to you. Compare your attempt with the correct version. Try to learn only those words which you have misspelled.

5. Focus on the letters you need to learn in each of the misspelled words. It is often useful to recopy the part of the word you spelled correctly and leave a blank space for each letter misspelled.

Correct	Misspelling	Recopy
bruise	broose	br_ _se
tension	tenshun	tens_ _n
channel	channal	chann_l

6. Use a variety of spelling strategies to study the words. Try a number of the suggestions in *Chapter 1: Spelling Strategies*.

7. Work with a partner and discuss which strategies may be most helpful for learning specific words.

8. When you study your list again, begin with the words you misspelled the previous time.

9. Make an effort to use these words in your everyday writing. Otherwise, they will not become a part of your natural spelling vocabulary.

LONG VOWEL PATTERNS

Vowel–consonant–e

a–e

airplane	forgave	replace
became	microwave	scale
debase	migrate	separate
escape	mistake	stage
female	nickname	

e–e

athlete	extreme
compete	these
complete	

i–e

admire	divide	provide
combine	excite	refine
concise	invite	reside
decide	knife	strife
decline	meanwhile	sunshine
define	otherwise	widely
describe	parasite	
dislike	prize	

o–e

compose	noteworthy	stroke
dispose	oppose	tadpole
homesick	propose	telephone
hopeful	quote	wholesome
lonely	rhinestone	

u–e

chute	dispute	perfume
conclude	flute	useful
consumer	opportune	

/ā/: ai, ay, eigh

ai

braid	maintain	remaining
drainage	painful	sailor
explain	painting	snail
failure	praise	tailor
faithful	raining	traitor
maiden	raised	waist
mailbox	regain	waiter

ay

bluejay	display	stray
crayon	highway	swaying
daylight	maybe	x–ray
delay	playmate	

eigh

neighbour
sleigh
weigh

/ē/: ee, ea, y, i

ee

agree	fifteen	referee
beehive	freedom	reindeer
between	gleefully	squeeze
creep	keepsake	tree house
degree	meeting	upkeep
eerie	needless	weekend
feelings	proceed	wheelbarrow

ea

eagle	neatness	seashore
ear	peanut	season
easel	pleading	teacup
easily	readable	teammate
eastern	really	weakling
feast	release	

y

already	gravity	scurry
bury	hurry	steady
everything	majority	thoroughly
family	opportunity	
frequently	salary	

Words in History: **Salary**—Part of a Roman soldier's pay was made in salt known as *salarium*.

i

audio	patio	radius
auditorium	piano	ratio
curiosity	pizza	ravioli
delirium	radio	spaghetti
opium	radium	studio

Wacky Definitions: How is a fish different than a piano? *You can't tuna fish*.

/ī/: igh

brightly	lightning	slight
firefighter	mighty	thigh
flight	nightmare	tightrope
frighten	sigh	
highlight	sightseeing	

/ō/: oa, ow, o

oa

boastful	meatloaf
coach	railroad
coastal	roadblock
goalie	toaster

ow

arrow	follow	snowball
below	growth	stowaway
borrow	owner	tomorrow
bowling	owing	yellow
crowbar	rowboat	

o

bingo	photo	tomato
echo	piano	video
hello	potato	volcano
hero	radio	zero
memo	solo	
patio	taco	

/ü/: ui, oo, ew

Pronounced /ü/ as in **boot** or /yü/ as in **cute**.

ui

bruise	nuisance
cruise	pursuit
fruit	suitable
juicy	

oo

baboon	cocoon	proofread
balloon	foolish	raccoon
cartoon	groove	shooting
choose	hooligan	spoon

Words in History: hooligan—The *Houlihan* family, which lived in London, England in the last century, was considered very wild.

ew

brewing	curfew	threw
cashew	jewels	withdrew
chewing	knew	
corkscrew	renew	

✓ Some rules for *long vowel patterns* can be found on pages 27–29.

DIPHTHONGS /OI/ AND /OU/

/oi/: oy, oi

oy

annoyed	deploy	joyful
boycott	destroy	unemployed
convoy	disloyal	voyage
corduroy	enjoyment	
decoy	envoy	

oi

appointment	exploit	rejoice
avoidance	moisture	sirloin
broiler	noisy	turmoil
choice	ointment	typhoid
disappoint	point	voice
embroider	poison	

/ou/: ou, ow

ou

about	crouch	ounce
accountant	discount	ourselves
aloud	doubtful	outfield
amount	foundation	outlook
around	grouchy	pronoun
boundary	hour	slouched
cloudy	loudness	surrounding
council	mountain	underground
county	ouch	

ow

allowance	eyebrow	scowl
chowder	flower	shower
clown	powder	somehow
crowded	powerful	towel
downtown	prowler	vowel

✓ Examples of the **/oi/** and **/ou/** patterns are discussed on page 30.

R–INFLUENCED VOWELS

/ėr/: ur, or, ir, er, ear

ur

burden	furnish	turtle
burst	further	urge
churn	murder	urgent
curve	purse	
disturb	pursue	

or

word	worship
world	worst
worm	worthy
worse	

ir

birthday	dirty	thirsty
circle	first	thirteen
circuit	girdle	whirl
circus	skirt	
confirm	third	

er

allergy	observe	reverse
battery	operate	sermon
camera	perhaps	serve
concern	person	stern
dangerous	persuade	verse
federal	preserve	
mercy	reserve	

ear

early	heard
earn	learn
earnest	search
earth	

✓ Look up this pattern in Chapter 2, pages 30–31, for a list of some spelling rules.

VARIATIONS ON CONSONANT SPELLINGS

/sh/: ci, sci, ti, ch, ss

ci

ancient	especially	politician
appreciate	financial	precious
commercial	gracious	sufficient
delicious	musician	suspicion
efficient	official	

sci

conscience
conscious
fascism
luscious

ti

confidential	partial
initial	patient
initiation	substantial

ch

chalet
chaperone
chic
crotchet
mustache

ss

mission
pressure
session

/ch/: t, tch

t

celestial	fortunate	situate
century	indigestion	situation
combustion	mutual	sumptuous
congestion	perpetual	spiritual
digestion	punctual	statute
eventual	question	suggestion
exhaustion	saturate	

tch

batch	dispatcher	ketchup
butcher	etching	kitchen
catcher	hatch	stitch
clutch	itchy	stretch

✓ Examples of the /**sh**/ and /**ch**/ pattern are found on pages 31–32.

EI AND IE WORDS

ie

achieve	fiery	priest
apiece	friendship	relief
belief	grieve	review
believe	handkerchief	shield
brief	hygiene	siege
chief	mischief	thief
diesel	niece	yield
field	piece	
fierce	pierce	

e after c

ceiling	perceive
conceit	receipt
conceive	receive
deceive	

/ā/

beige	veil
eighth	vein
freight	weigh
neighbour	weight
reign	

✓ Turn to page 33 for some of the rules of *EI and IE* words.

SILENT LETTERS

silent t: st, ft

st

bristle	gristle	rustle
bustle	hasten	thistle
castle	hustle	whistle
chestnut	listen	wrestle
fasten	moisten	wrestler
glisten	nestle	

ft

often
soften

silent g: gh, gn

gh

although	fought	taught
bought	fright	though
brought	midnight	thought
caught	ought	thorough
daughter	slight	through
dough	sought	twilight
flight	straight	

gn

align	gnash	resign
assign	gnat	sign
design	gnaw	

silent b: mb

bomb	dumb	plumber
climb	lamb	thumb
comb	limb	tomb
crumb	numb	

silent u: ua, ue, ui

ua

guarantee
guard
guardian

ue

guess
guest

ui

biscuit	guide
building	guilty
built	guitar
disguise	

silent l: lm, lk

lm

calm
palm
salmon

lk

folk	talkative
folklore	yolk
stalk	

silent k: kn

knack	knitting
knapsack	knob
knee	knock
kneel	knowledge
knife	knot
knight	knuckle

/r/ sound

silent h: rh

rhyme
rhythm

silent w: wr

wrestle
wrinkle

✓ If you want more help understanding these *silent letters*, turn to pages 34–35.

UNSTRESSED ENDINGS

/əl/: le, al, el

le

bundle	needle	sample
chuckle	nozzle	settle
dazzle	pickle	single
double	puzzle	stumble
grumble	riddle	struggle
handle	saddle	wrinkle

al

actual	legal	personal
animal	local	political
annual	medical	principal
capital	mental	rural
carnival	metal	several
central	mineral	signal
crystal	moral	substantial
dual	musical	testimonial
equal	normal	total
eternal	original	usual
identical	pedal	
final	pedestal	

el

angel	chapel	parcel
barrel	duel	sentinel
bushel	easel	shovel
camel	level	shrivel
cancel	nickel	travel
channel	panel	tunnel

/ėr/: er, or, ar

er

blister	eager	silver
chatter	glider	slender
container	hunger	thunder
dealer	litter	trailer
deliver	panther	

or

actor	governor	senator
alligator	horror	spectator
author	major	sponsor
competitor	mayor	terror
director	mirror	tractor
doctor	motor	tenor
editor	sailor	
error	scissors	

Back-up singer: The leader of our rock group says I should sing tenor.
Guitarist: Tenor?
Back-up singer: Yeah, *ten or* twelve kilometres away!

ar

beggar	grammar	polar
burglar	hangar	popular
calendar	liar	regular
cedar	molar	scholar
cellar	nuclear	similar
collar	particular	spectacular
dollar	peculiar	vinegar
familiar	pillar	

/ən/: in, en, on, ain

in

cabin	raisin
cousin	robin
margin	

en

darken	glisten	listen
even	hasten	straighten
fasten	kitchen	strengthen
frighten	linen	sunken

on

bacon	melon	reason
carbon	mutton	ribbon
gallon	pardon	season
lesson	poison	weapon

ain

captain	fountain
certain	mountain
curtain	

/ət/: it, et, ot, ate

it

credit	habit	spirit
deposit	limit	unit
digit	orbit	visit

et

banquet	faucet	nugget
bullet	ferret	scarlet
closet	hatchet	socket
diet	midget	

ot

ballot	pilot
bigot	riot
carrot	zealot
parrot	

ate

climate	fortunate
delicate	frigate
duplicate	private

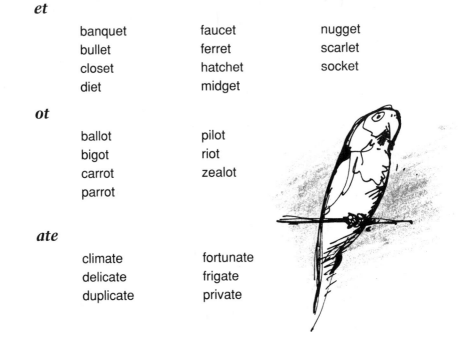

✓ The /ėr/, /it/, and /ən/ patterns are covered in
Spelling Patterns on pages 36–37.

COMPOUND WORDS

Compound word	**Comes from**
birthplace	birth + place
blueprint	blue + print
bookkeeper	book + keeper
cardboard	card + board
carefree	care + free

Compound word	Comes from
daylight	day + light
doughnut	dough + nut
earring	ear + ring
earthquake	earth + quake
everyone	every + one
everything	every + thing
extraordinary	extra + ordinary
farewell	fare + well
fireproof	fire + proof
flashlight	flash + light
forehead	fore + head
frostbite	frost + bite
glowworm	glow + worm
granddaughter	grand + daughter
haircut	hair + cut
headache	head + ache
hitchhike	hitch + hike
homework	home + work
jackknife	jack + knife
loudspeaker	loud + speaker
marshmallow	marsh + mallow
meanwhile	mean + while
nevertheless	never + the + less
newspaper	news + paper
nighttime	night + time
nowhere	no + where
otherwise	other + wise
overseas	over + seas
paperback	paper + back
pineapple	pine + apple
rattlesnake	rattle + snake
roommate	room + mate
safeguard	safe + guard
sideburns	side + burns

Compound word	Comes from
sidewalk	side + walk
skateboard	skate + board
skyscraper	sky + scraper
snowmobile	snow + mobile
somebody	some + body
suitcase	suit + case
teammate	team + mate
teenage	teen + age
throughout	through + out
toothbrush	tooth + brush
typewriter	type + writer
upright	up + right
uproar	up + roar
viewpoint	view + point
volleyball	volley + ball
wastebasket	waste + basket
whatever	what + ever
windshield	wind + shield
withhold	with + hold
worthwhile	worth + while

Words in History: Sideburns—side-whiskers were named after the American Civil War general Ambrose Everett *Burnside* (1824–81).

✓ Look up this pattern in Chapter 2, on page 38, if you need more help.

CONTRACTIONS

don't	do not
hadn't	had not
hasn't	has not
haven't	have not
he'd	he would, he had
here's	here is
it'll	it will
mustn't	must not
she'd	she would, she had
shouldn't	should not
that's	that is
they'll	they will
they've	they have
you'd	you would, you had
they'd	they would, they had
you've	you have
we'd	we would, we had
where's	where is
who's	who is

✓ Rules for some of the *contractions* are on page 39.

PLURALS

Regular: add –s

antonyms	promises
changes	skis
forests	strangers
messages	synonyms
orchards	uniforms

Nouns ending with s, sh, ch, and x: add –es

s

actresses	glasses
addresses	octopuses
circuses	surpluses
compasses	

sh

toothbrushes
eyelashes

ch

beaches	scratches
branches	speeches
sandwiches	

x

prefixes
reflexes
saxes
suffixes

Words in History: Saxophone(sax)—Antoine–Joseph *Sax* (1814–94) invented the saxophone.

Nouns ending with y

Preceded by vowel: add –s

alleys	journeys	turkeys
attorneys	kidneys	valleys
chimneys	monkeys	
donkeys	pulleys	

Preceded by a consonant: change y to i and add –es

allergies	dairies	policies
allies	diaries	skies
assemblies	enemies	territories
biographies	juries	theories
centuries	libraries	trophies
cities	luxuries	
countries	pastries	

Nouns ending with o: add –s

banjos	photos	studios
dynamos	pianos	tacos
memos	radios	videos
patios	rodeos	zeros (or zeroes)

Wacky Definition: *kid*neys.

Nouns ending with f or fe: add –s

beliefs	giraffes	scarfs
chiefs	handkerchiefs	sheriffs
dwarfs	roofs	wharfs

Many exceptions

calves	leaves	shelves
elves	lives	thieves
halves	loaves	wives
knives	selves	wolves

Do you see a pattern in the exceptions?

✓ Many of the rules for making *plurals* are covered on pages 40–44.

SPECIAL PLURAL FORMS

Irregular forms

children
men
women

Words ending with –*ful*: add –s

cupfuls
handfuls

Letters, numbers, and words: add 's

the 1990's
three v's
five 6's
three and's

Proper nouns: add –s or –es

the Ashtons
the Howiches
the Murphys

Nouns which keep their Latin plural form

Singular	Plural
analysis	analyses
crisis	crises
criterion	criteria
diagnosis	diagnoses
datum	data
hypothesis	hypotheses
medium	media
phenomenon	phenomena

✓ Turn to pages 44–46 in *Chapter 2: Spelling Patterns* if you need more help.

Words in History: ritz, ritzy—Cesar Ritz (1850–1918) had a string of very expensive hotels: the *Ritz Hotels*.

POSSESSIVES

Singular nouns like *child*: add 's

artist's	doctor's	niece's
author's	girl's	person's
baby's	goalie's	referee's
chef's	grandfather's	witness's
child's	hotel's	uncle's
daughter's	magician's	

Plural nouns like *men*: add 's

children's
men's
women's

Plural nouns already ending in s, like *girls*: add '

citizens'
goalies'
judges'
opponents'
partners'
players'
students'

✓ Single and plural *possessives* are examined in detail on pages 45–47.

ADDING ENDINGS: Y TO I

Adding *-ed* and *-ing*

Base word	Add *-ed*	Add *-ing*
apply	applied	applying
bury	buried	burying
classify	classified	classifying
deny	denied	denying
justify	justified	justifying
magnify	magnified	magnifying
marry	married	marrying
multiply	multiplied	multiplying
notify	notified	notifying
occupy	occupied	occupying
pity	pitied	pitying
rely	relied	relying
reply	replied	replying
satisfy	satisfied	satisfying
signify	signified	signifying
specify	specified	specifying
supply	supplied	supplying
testify	testified	testifying

Adding other endings

Base word	With ending
angry	angrily
busy	busily
clumsy	clumsiness
costly	costliest
cosy	cosier
dizzy	dizziness
duty	dutiful
empty	emptiness

Base word	With ending
envy	envious
fancy	fanciful
friendly	friendliness
funny	funniest
fury	furious
gloomy	gloomiest
glory	glorious
greedy	greediness
happy	happiness
heavy	heavily
hungry	hungrily
lonely	loneliness
lucky	luckily
magnify	magnified
mercy	merciful
merry	merrily
modify	modified
mystery	mysterious
pity	pitiful
plenty	plentiful
qualify	qualified
steady	steadily
study	studious
vary	various
worthy	worthiness

Forming plurals

city	cities
dairy	dairies
enemy	enemies
grocery	groceries
lily	lilies
memory	memories
security	securities

✓ Look up these spelling rules of *Y to I endings* on pages 48–49.

SUFFIXES AND SILENT E

Suffixes beginning with a vowel

Base word	With suffix
admire	admirable
advise	advising
approve	approval
argue	arguing
arrange	arranging
arrive	arrival
become	becoming
choose	choosing
continue	continuing
desire	desirable
encourage	encouraging
excite	excitable
excuse	excusable
fame	famous
guide	guidance
hire	hiring
hope	hoping
ice	icy
juice	juicy
noise	noisy
propose	proposal
remove	removal
rise	rising
scare	scary
scribble	scribbled
separate	separating
shine	shining
smuggle	smuggled
solve	solved

Base word	With suffix
spice	spicy
tackle	tackled
tease	teasing
tide	tidal
use	using
value	valuable
wave	wavy
write	writing

Wacky Definitions: **icing**—*What I do in the shower*.

Suffixes beginning with a consonant

Base word	With suffix
absolute	absolutely
achieve	achievement
advertise	advertisement
announce	announcement
appropriate	appropriately
arrange	arrangement
brave	bravely
care	careful
close	closely
complete	completely
definite	definitely
engage	engagement
entire	entirely
excite	excitement
extreme	extremely
hope	hopeful
immediate	immediately
improve	improvement
infinite	infinitely
involve	involvement
late	lately
like	likely

Base word	With suffix
lone	lonely
manage	management
move	movement
nine	ninety
pave	pavement
peace	peaceful
pure	purely
resource	resourceful
safe	safety
severe	severely
sincere	sincerely
state	statement

✓ Examples of this pattern are discussed on pages 50–51.

DOUBLING BEFORE SUFFIXES

Single syllable words

Base word	–ed	–ing
blur	blurred	blurring
clog	clogged	clogging
cram	crammed	cramming
fit	fitted	fitting
flip	flipped	flipping
jut	jutted	jutting
knit	knitted	knitting
map	mapped	mapping
rob	robbed	robbing
scar	scarred	scarring
shrug	shrugged	shrugging
slam	slammed	slamming
slip	slipped	slipping

Two syllable words

Base word	–ed	–ing	+suffix

Stress on 1st syllable

benefit	benefited	benefiting	
differ	differed	differing	difference
happen	happened	happening	
honour	honoured	honouring	honourable
limit	limited		limitless
listen	listened	listening	
pardon	pardoned	pardoning	pardoner
pilot	piloted	piloting	pilotage
profit	profited	profiting	profitless
reason	reasoned	reasoning	reasonable
rumour	rumoured		

Stress on 2nd syllable

acquit	acquitted	acquitting	
begin		beginning	beginner
commit	committed	committing	commitment
confer	conferred	conferring	conference
control	controlled	controlling	
equip	equipped	equipping	equipment
expel	expelled	expelling	
forbid		forbidding	forbidden
forget		forgetting	forgetful
occur	occurred	occurring	occurrence

Base word	–ed	–ing	+suffix
omit	omitted	omitting	
patrol	patrolled	patrolling	
prefer	preferred	preferring	preference
propel	propelled	propelling	propeller
refer	referred	referring	reference
regret	regretted	regretting	regretful
repel	repelled	repelling	repellent

✓ Turn to pages 52–53 if you need more help with this pattern.

OTHER DOUBLING PATTERNS

Double letters with prefixes

accept	appointment	irrigation
accident	approach	misspelled
accompany	assembly	misstated
accomplish	attending	reelect
according	attention	reexamine
accountant	attorney	successful
accuracy	attraction	suggestion
accuse	co–operate	surrender
address	dissatisfy	surround
affectionate	dissolve	unnatural
aggravate	immediate	unnoticed
appeal	immortal	
appearance	immunity	

✓ *Other doubling patterns* are discussed on pages 54–55.

RELATED WORDS

/t/ to /sh/

Base word	Related word
detect	detection
duplicate	duplication
exhibit	exhibition
generate	generation
investigate	investigation
operate	operation
participate	participation
punctuate	punctuation
recollect	recollection
violate	violation

Long vowel to short

Base word	Related word
arise	arisen
athlete	athletic
daze	dazzle
extreme	extremity
flame	flammable
global	globular
grateful	gratitude
grave	gravity
humane	humanity
ignite	ignition
microscope	microscopic
nation	national
nature	natural
precise	precision
prescribe	prescription

Base word	Related word
produce	production
provide	provision
reduce	reduction
revise	revision
severe	severity
televise	television
volcano	volcanic

Long or short vowel to schwa

Base word	Related word
admire	admiration
adapt	adaptation
adore	adoration
advantage	advantageous
agile	agility
civilian	civilize
combine	combination
comedian	comedy
compete	competition
compose	composition
confer	conference
confide	confident
contribute	contribution
decide	decision
declare	declaration
define	definition
design	designation
demolish	demolition
deprive	deprivation
dispose	disposition
divide	dividend
ecology	ecological
editor	editorial
excel	excellent
expose	exposition
fatal	fatality

final	finality
habit	habitat
harmony	harmonious
history	historical
hospital	hospitality
impose	imposition
incline	inclination
inflammable	inflammation
inform	information
inspire	inspiration
install	installation
invite	invitation
major	majority
memo	memorandum
narrate	narrative
oblige	obligation
oppose	opposition
organize	organization
politics	political
popular	popularity
prepare	preparation
preserve	preservation
prohibit	prohibition
propose	proposition
reform	reformation
regular	regularity
reside	resident
resolve	resolution
specific	specify
stable	stability

Schwa to long or short vowel

Base word	Related word
general	generality
moral	morality
normal	normality
origin	original
personal	personality
remedy	remedial

Silent consonant to sounded

Base word	Related word
autumn	autumnal
bomb	bombard
column	columnist
condemn	condemnation
design	designation
fiction	fictitious
hymn	hymnal
muscle	muscular
resign	resignation
sign	signature

✓ If you need help understanding these patterns, turn to pages 55–58.

HOMOPHONES

allowed	aloud
bare	bear
base	bass
board	bored
border	boarder
break	brake
chili	chilly
course	coarse
died	dyed
fair	fare
forth	fourth
fir	fur

grate	great	
hangar	hanger	
heard	herd	
led	lead	
main	mane	
pail	pale	
pain	pane	
pair	pare	pear
pore	pour	
principal	principle	
rain	reign	
scent	sent	
seen	scene	
some	sum	
steak	stake	
stationary	stationery	
there	their	they're
through	threw	
to	two	too
tax	tacks	
vain	vein	
waist	waste	
wait	weight	
ware	wear	
week	weak	
whose	who's	

✓ A discussion of *homophone* patterns can be found on page 59.

FRENCH WORDS IN ENGLISH

English word	Comes from	Meaning
antique	*antique*	very old
ballet	*ballet*	a dance
banquet	*banquet*	a feast
boulevard	*boulevard*	a wide street
bouquet	*bouquet*	a bunch of flowers
buffet	*buffet*	refreshment bar
camouflage	*camoufler*	disguise
career	*carriere*	a race course
caterpillar	*catepelose*	a hairy cat
chandelier	*chandelier*	a candle
chowder	*chaudiere*	a kettle
chute	*chute*	fall
cocoon	*cocon*	a shell
corsage	*cors*	bodice
coupon	*coupon*	piece cut off
crayon	*crayon*	a pencil
crochet	*crochet*	a small hook
croquet	*croquet*	a hooked stick
depose	*deposer*	lay down, remove
detour	*detour*	a detour
emerald	*esmeraude*	an emerald
etiquette	*etiquette*	a ticket
fatigue	*fatiguer*	weary
garage	*garer*	take care
gauge	*gauge*	fixed measure
gopher	*gaufre*	a honeycomb
lacrosse	*la crosse*	hooked stick
lieutenant	*lieutenant*	a lieutenant
macrame	*macrame*	a fringe of knotted cord

English word	Comes from	Meaning
massage	*masser*	massage
mirage	*mirage*	mirage
picturesque	*pittoresque*	picturesque
pigeon	*pijon*	young dove
pioneer	*pionnier*	soldier going ahead of an army to prepare the way
plateau	*plateau*	something flat
porpoise	*porpois*	a porpoise
portrait	*portrait*	portrait
poultry	*pouleterie*	little chickens
prairie	*prairie*	a large meadow
promenade	*promenade*	walk
quail	*quaille*	quail
rapport	*rapporter*	bring again
restaurant	*restaurant*	a restaurant

LATIN ROOTS

Dict: from the verb *dicere*, meaning "to say"

contradiction	indictment
dictator	predicament
dictionary	prediction

Duc: from the verb *ducere*, meaning "to lead"

deduction	producer
inducement	productivity
introductory	viaduct

Junct: from the verb *jungere*, meaning "to join"

injunction
junction

Mit: from the verb *mittere*, meaning "to send"

admittance	emission	submit
commit	intermission	transmitter
dismissal	permissible	

Pend: from the verb *pendere*, meaning "to weigh"

appendix	expenditure
compensation	pension
dependable	suspend

Plic: from the verb *plicare*, meaning "to fold"

applicable	duplicator
complicate	implication
complication	replica

Plor: from the verb *plorare*, meaning "to weep aloud"

>   deplorable
>   explorer
>   implore

Press: from the verb *premere*, meaning "to press"

>   compression   impressive
>   depress   oppressor
>   expressive

Rupt: from the verb *rumpere*, meaning "to break"

>   corruption   rupture
>   disrupt   uninterrupted
>   eruption

Scribe: from the verb *scribere*, meaning "to write"

>   description   inscription
>   inscribe   subscription

Sent: from the verb *sentire*, meaning "to feel"

>   insensitive   sentimental
>   sensible   sentry
>   sensitivity

Sist: from the verb *sistere*, meaning "to stand firm"

>   insistent
>   persistence
>   resist

Spect: from the verb *spectare*, meaning "to look"

>   expectation   spectacle
>   inspector   spectacular
>   prospector   spectator

Spir: from the verb *spirare*, meaning "to breathe"

- aspiration
- conspiracy
- expire
- perspiration
- respiration

Struct: from the verb *struere*, meaning "to build"

- destructible
- destructive
- instructor
- obstruction
- structure
- reconstruct

Vers: from the verb *vertere*, meaning "to turn"

- converse
- diverse
- reverse

Vert: from the verb *vertere*, meaning "to turn"

- convert
- divert
- extrovert
- revert
- vertical

Voc: from the verb *vocare*, meaning "to call"

- advocate
- revoke
- vocabulary
- vocal
- vocalize

Volv: from the verb *volvere*, meaning "to turn or to roll"

- evolve
- involved
- revolution
- revolve

✓ For a more detailed look at *Latin roots*, turn to page 63.

GREEK WORDS IN ENGLISH

English word	Comes from
atheist	*atheos*
atomic	*atomos*
authentic	*authentikos*
autobiography	*autos + biog*
autograph	*autographon*
biology	*biology*
chameleon	*khamaileon*
chronic	*khronikos*
chronometer	*khronos + meter*
crystal	*krystallos*
cyclone	*kukloma*
eclipse	*ekleipsis*
elastic	*elastikos*
epidemic	*epidemia*
geography	*geographia*
geology	*geology*
hippopotamus	*hippopotamos*
metaphor	*metaphora*
monarchy	*monarkhos*
monopoly	*monopolion*
monotonous	*monotonos*
pantomime	*pantomimos*
parasite	*parasitos*
photography	*photo + graphos*
physician	*physike*
rhinoceros	*rhinokeros*
schedule	*schidē*

English word	Comes from
skeleton	*skeleton*
static	*statikos*
sympathy	*sumpatheia*
symphony	*sumphonia*
system	*systema*
telephone	*tele + phone*
theology	*theologia*
thermometer	*therme + meter*
thermostat	*thermo + statos*

Words in History: **crocodile** comes from the Greek word, *krokodeilos*, meaning "worm of the stones." In ancient times, crocodiles had a habit of resting on pebbly banks.

✓ This pattern can be found in ***Chapter 2: Spelling Patterns*** on page 64.

PREFIXES: NEGATION

in–

inability	inconsiderate	inexpensive
inaccurate	inconvenient	inexperienced
incapable	indefinite	

il–

illegal
illegible
illiteracy

ir–

irregular	irresistible
irrelevant	irresponsible

im–

imbalance	immovable	impure
immature	imperfect	
immortal	improper	

un–

unbearable	uneducated	unknown
uncertain	unemployment	unnatural
uncommon	unexpected	unnecessary
undecided	unfortunately	unpopular

non–

non–profit	non–returnable
non–resident	nonsense

dis–

disabled	discontinue	disloyal
disagreement	discount	disobey
disappear	discouraged	disrespectful
disapprove	discredited	dissatisfied
disassemble	disfigured	distasteful
disbelief	disgraceful	
disconnect	dishonest	

✓ These prefix patterns are discussed on pages 66–67.

PREFIXES: NUMBER

uni–: one

unicorn	union	universal
unification	unique	universe
uniform	unison	university
unify	unite	

bi–: twice, double, two

biannual	bicycle	binomial
bicentennial	bifocal	bisect
biceps	bigamy	biweekly
biculturalism	bimonthly	

tri–: three

triad	trillium	triplane
triangle	trilogy	triple
tricolour	trimester	triplets
tricycle	trinomial	triplicate
trident	trio	tripod

semi–: half, partly

semi–annual	semidetached	semiskilled
semicircle	semifinal	semitone
semicolon	semiformal	semitropical
semiconscious	semiprecious	

✓ *Number prefixes* can be found in **Chapter 2: Spelling Patterns** on pages 67–68.

PREFIXES: OPPOSITES

pre–/post–
pre–: before

preamble	predetermine	preliminary
prearrange	predictable	premature
precaution	prefabricated	premier
precede	preface	premonition
precedent	prefix	prenatal
preconceived	prehistoric	preview
precondition	prejudge	previous
predecessor	prejudice	

post–: after

postdate	posthumous	postpone
posterior	postlude	postscript
posterity	postnatal	postwar
postgraduate	post–operative	

pro-/anti-

pro-: forward, in favour of, before

procedure	professional	prolong
proceed	proficient	promotion
process	profound	propeller
proclaim	progress	proposition
procreate	projector	protrude
production	prologue	provoke

anti-: against, the opposite of, preventing

anti-aircraft	antifreeze	antisocial
antibody	antigens	antitoxin
anticlimax	antihistamine	
antidote	antiseptic	

✓ A more detailed look at this pattern can be found on pages 68–69.

PREFIXES: DIRECTION

trans-: across, over, down, or beyond

transaction	transfusion	transparent
transcontinental	transistor	transplant
transcript	transition	transportation
transfer	translation	
transform	transmit	

sub–: under or beneath

subcommittee	subliminal	subsistence
subconscious	submarine	substitute
subcontractor	submerge	subtraction
subdivide	subnormal	suburban
subdue	subordinate	
subheading	subscription	

inter–: between or among

interaction	interject	interracial
interception	interlocking	interrupt
interchange	intermediate	intersection
intercollegiate	intermission	interval
intercom	international	interview
interdependent	interplanetary	
interfere	interpret	

✓ If you need help learning these patterns, turn to pages 69–70.

SUFFIXES: NOUN SUFFIXES

–ness

awareness	consciousness	loneliness
bitterness	forgetfulness	seriousness
carelessness	friendliness	
cheerfulness	happiness	

–dom

boredom	martyrdom
freedom	wisdom
kingdom	

–ment

accomplishment	equipment	requirement
argument	entertainment	temperament
arrangement	harassment	
disappointment	judgment	

–ian

comedian	librarian	physician
custodian	magician	politician
electrician	mathematician	
historian	musician	

–er

bartender	lecturer	programmer
biker	manager	researcher
labourer	plumber	teacher

–or

actor	creator	mediator
adjudicator	decorator	moderator
conductor	director	spectator
contractor	divisor	

–ure/–ture

adventure	indenture	rapture
architecture	legislature	scripture
creature	literature	sculpture
culture	mixture	signature
departure	moisture	temperature
expenditure	nature	texture
fixture	overture	
forfeiture	posture	

–ion

complexion
opinion
pinion

–sion

admission	emission	persuasion
collision	erosion	possession
commission	explosion	profession
compression	expression	provision
conclusion	fusion	revision
concussion	immersion	succession
confession	impression	suspension
confusion	invasion	television
decision	obsession	transfusion
depression	permission	

–tion

absorption	connection	duplication
action	construction	edition
affection	convention	ejection
anticipation	correction	election
attraction	defection	evacuation
collection	demonstration	exhibition
completion	description	infection
concentration	detection	inflation
conception	direction	initiation

inspection	objection	reflection
instruction	operation	relation
insulation	option	satisfaction
intention	perfection	situation
introduction	population	station
invention	production	termination
legislation	recognition	traction
location	reduction	

–ation

admiration	examination	plantation
anticipation	foundation	registration
cancellation	imagination	representation
civilization	information	reservation
combination	inspiration	specification
confirmation	installation	starvation
conversation	multiplication	taxation
declaration	occupation	

–ition

abolition	demolition	repetition
addition	opposition	requisition
competition	preposition	transition
composition	prohibition	
definition	recognition	

✓ Pages 70–71 will give you more help in learning these patterns.

SUFFIXES: ADJECTIVE OR NOUN SUFFIXES

–ible

accessible	flexible	reversible
digestible	forcible	sensible
exhaustible	responsible	

–able

acceptable	comfortable	inflammable
available	considerable	memorable
believable	dependable	taxable
biodegradable	excusable	
changeable	fashionable	

–ery

archery	flattery	misery
artery	forgery	scenery
bravery	jewellery	slavery
drapery	lottery	
embroidery	machinery	

–ary

adversary	fragmentary	revolutionary
boundary	honourary	secondary
commentary	imaginary	secretary
customary	planetary	summary
dictionary	primary	visionary

−*ory*

advisory	inventory
circulatory	laboratory
explanatory	sensory

−*ous*

ambiguous	famous	nervous
barbarous	glamorous	prosperous
bulbous	hazardous	ridiculous
cancerous	joyous	scandalous
continuous	marvellous	studious
disastrous	mischievous	treacherous
enormous	mountainous	vigorous

−*ious*

barbarious	glorious	rebellious
commodious	harmonious	spacious
conscientious	luxurious	studious
felonious	melodious	victorious
furious	mysterious	

✓ If you need help understanding these patterns, turn
to pages 72–73.

OTHER ENDINGS

–ent/–ence

–ent	*–ence*
absent	absence
adolescent	adolescence
competent	competence
confident	confidence
convenient	convenience
dependent	dependence
different	difference
evident	evidence
excellent	excellence
independent	independence
innocent	innocence
magnificent	magnificence
obedient	obedience
patient	patience
permanent	permanence
present	presence
prominent	prominence
resident	residence
silent	silence
violent	violence

–ant/–ance

–ant	–ance
abundant	abundance
attendant	attendance
distant	distance
dominant	dominance
elegant	elegance
fragrant	fragrance
ignorant	ignorance
instant	instance
observant	observance
radiant	radiance
resistant	resistance
significant	significance
tolerant	tolerance

Word Quiz: What is the best smelling ant? *Fragrant*. What is the brightest ant? *Radiant*. What is the quickest ant? *Instant*.

–ise

advertise	disguise	revise
advise	enterprise	supervise
compromise	exercise	surprise
despise	improvise	
devise	merchandise	

–ize

apologize	harmonize	penalize
authorize	hypnotize	realize
baptize	industrialize	recognize
characterize	itemize	specialize
civilize	legalize	symbolize
criticize	mechanize	sympathize
economize	memorize	vaporize
emphasize	modernize	visualize
fertilize	organize	
generalize	pasteurize	

–ise/–yze

analyse/analyze
paralyse/paralyze

The ending **–ise/–yze** is very *uncommon* in English spelling. Can you think of any other words with this ending?

✓ Turn to pages 73–74 for some rules which might help you with these endings.

Chapter 8
Further Investigations

INTRODUCTION

The activities in this section have been written to test your understanding of the spelling patterns presented in Chapter 2. If you find some of the activities difficult, go back to the same pattern section in Chapter 2 and read the information carefully. You may wish to test your understanding more fully with other words of this type in *Chapter 7: Word Lists*. Finally, the proofreading passage in Chapter 3, based on each pattern, will show whether you are able to discover these types of errors in the context of a paragraph.

Use the *Self–analysis Checklist* on pages 8–9 to help find the page numbers of a specific pattern with which you are having difficulty.

196

LONG VOWEL PATTERNS

Vowel–consonant–e

A The following words all contain long vowels based on the **vowel–consonant–e** pattern, as in **scale**.

1. Write each word with the correct letters.

extr_m_	pr_vid_	teleph_n_
descr_b_	h_p_ful	microw_v_
repl_c_	disp_t_	athl_t_
meanwh_l_	paras_t_	concl_d_

Other long vowel patterns

B Complete the following sentences with words which have the required long vowel sound.

/ā/

1. It was difficult to expl_ _n why the warning lights f_ _led to work at the r_ _lway crossing.
2. The child shared her brightly coloured cr_ _ons and p_ _nts with her pl_ _mates.

/ē/

3. The refer_ _ at last w_ _kend's hock_ _ game had trouble k_ _ping the majorit_ of players from fighting.
4. The artist's stud_o had ever_thing I r_ _ll_ n_ _ded to proc_ _d with my work.

/ī/

5. Seeing the br_ _ _tly lit l_ _ _ts of the city was the h_ _ _l_ _ _t of our s_ _ _tseeing fl_ _ _t over the region.
6. The f_r_f_ _ _ters had the fr_ _ _tening experience of tr_ing to put out the many f_r_s set by l_ _ _tning.

Chapter 8 FURTHER INVESTIGATIONS

/ō/

7. The c_ _ch declared that our g_ _lie was the her_ of the game.

8. The roaring winds of the tornad_ knocked out radi_ contact with c_ _stal areas, damaged the railr_ _ds, and caused rivers to _verfl_ _ their banks.

/ū/

9. The n_ _spaper withdr_ _ the cart_ _n because it was uns_ _table for the children's page.

10. The rac_ _n was quite a n_ _sance because it ch_wed thr_ _ _ _ the screen trying to find j_ _cy fr_ _t and other kinds of f_ _d.

DIPHTHONGS

A The following words contain the sound /oi/, as in **boy**. This sound is usually spelled **oi** or **oy**. Complete each word with the correct pattern.

v_yage	ann_ _ed	empl_ _ment
rej_ _ce	disl_ _al	p_ _son
_ _ntment	typh_ _d	cordur_ _
destr_ _	av_ _dance	b_ _cott
disapp_ _nt	env_ _	m_ _sture

B Now try the sentences with words containing the /ou/ sound, as in **town**. This sound is usually spelled **ou** or **ow**.

1. The acc_ _ntant informed the t_ _n c_ _ncil that the financial _ _tlook was not very positive.

2. The p_ _erful volcanic eruption shook the m_ _ntain and the surr_ _nding areas, and sent a sh_ _er of ash into the sky. The black cl_ _d spread over the c_ _nty and turned the cr_ _ded d_ _ntown section of a nearby city into a state of panic.

R–INFLUENCED VOWELS

A The sound /ėr/ as in **bird** is spelled a number of ways. It is spelled **ur** in **curve**, **or** in **word**, **ir** in **bird**, **er** in **stern**, and **ear** in **earn**.

B Put in the correct spelling of /ėr/ in the words below. Check with a dictionary if you need help.

f_rnish	w_rld	c_rcle
_ _rnest	th_rsty	f_rther
dist_rb	all_rgy	s_ _rch
pres_rve	h_ _rd	m_rder
w_rthy	c_rcuit	w_rship
conf_rm	p_rhaps	_ _rly
res_rve	th_rteen	t_rtle
_rgent	c_rcus	w_rst
dang_rous	l_ _rn	wh_rl
g_rdle	p_rsue	p_rsuade

VARIATIONS ON CONSONANT SPELLINGS

/sh/

The sound /sh/ has six common spellings: **ci** in **ancient**, **sh** in **cashew**, **sci** in **luscious**, **ti** in **initial**, **ch** in **chalet**, and **ss** in **mission**.

A Complete the following words with the correct spelling of /**sh**/.

musi_ _an	pre_ _ure	_ _ampagne
ini_ _al	effi_ _ent	se_ _ion
musta_ _e	con_ _ _ence	confiden_ _al
politi_ _an	ini_ _ation	_ _alet
appre_ _ate	commer_ _al	con_ _ _ous
substan_ _al	suffi_ _ent	suspi_ _on
pa_ _ent	_ _ic	espe_ially

/ch/

The sound /**ch**/ is sometimes spelled **t** as in **mutual** or **tch** as in **kitchen**.

A Which spelling should you use? Rewrite the sentences with the correct spelling of the /**ch**/ sounds.

1. The ques_ion is, who spilled the ke_ _ _up all over the ki_ _ _en floor?
2. The unfor_unate si_uation could have been avoided if they had listened to his sugges_ion.
3. The pi_ _ _er and ca_ _ _er both stre_ _ _ed their legs and waited in the dugout until the rain even_ually ended.

EI AND IE WORDS

Remember the rule for spelling most **ei** and **ie** words:
Put **i** before **e**
Except after **c**,
Or when sounded like **ā**
As in neighbour and weigh

A Choose between **ei** and **ie** when completing the following words.

pr_ _st	c_ _ling	ach_ _ve
_ _ghth	fr_ _ndship	bel_ _ve
rec_ _ve	misch_ _f	r_ _gn
d_ _sel	rev_ _w	conc_ _ve
f_ _rce	perc_ _ve	sh_ _ld

B Now try these sentences with the correct letter combination.

1. The th_ _f stole an expensive p_ _ce of jewellery from my n_ _ghbour when she left her purse unattended for a br_ _f moment.
2. The y_ _ld of corn from that f_ _ld w_ _ghed several hundred kilograms per hectare.
3. In some countries v_ _ls are worn over the faces of female mourners during the gr_ _ving period following the death of a loved one.

C Here are some exceptions to the **ei** and **ie** rules. Do you know these words?

l_ _sure	spec_ _s	h_ _ght
consc_ _nce	for_ _gn	n_ _ther
forf_ _t	s_ _ze	w_ _rd

SILENT LETTERS

A Supply the missing **silent letters** for each word below.

cas_le	ou_ _t	sof_en
resi_n	plum_er	bisc_it
sa_mon	_nowledge	_rinkle
_nife	fo_klore	b_ilding
ca_m	tom_	assi_n
com_	g_arantee	pa_m
ta_kative	_nuckle	_res_le
_night	yo_k	disg_ise
dum_	desi_n	r_yme
_neel	r_ythm	g_ilty

UNSTRESSED ENDINGS

A The word ending /l/ or /əl/ can be spelled **le** as in **trouble**, **el** as in **camel**, or **al** as in **dial**.

1. Use the correct spelling pattern in this paragraph.

In the window of the toy shop were wooden puzz_ _s, cryst_ _ ornaments, music_ _ instruments, an artist's eas_ _, stuffed anim_ _s, and sever_ _ colourful parc_ _s. In one corner, an electric train chugged past a lev_ _ crossing, and disappeared into a tunn_ _.

B The final sound /ẻr/ can be spelled **er** as in **blister, or** as in **actor**, or **ar** as in **dollar**.

2. Complete each word below with the correct spelling of /ẻr/:

trail_ _	alligat_ _	burgl_ _
spectat_ _	spectacul_ _	contain_ _
competit_ _	panth_ _	direct_ _
calend_ _	nucle_ _	sciss_ _s
trait_ _	deliv_ _	famili_ _

C The final sound /it/ or /ət/ can be spelled **it** as in **orbit**, **et** as in **midget**, **ot** as in **ballot**, or **ate** as in **climate**.

1. Sort the words below into four columns according to their spelling of the sound /it/ or /ət/:

it (orbit)	et (midget)	ot (ballot)	ate (climate)
bull_ _	idi_ _	priv_ _ _	banqu_ _
depos_ _	delic_ _ _	fauc_ _	parr_ _
carr_ _	nugg_ _	spir_ _	dig_ _
pil_ _	fortun_ _ _	big_ _	

D The final sound /in/ or /ən/ is spelled **in** in **cabin, en** in **darken, on** in **melon**, and **ain** in **curtain**.

1. Which spelling is correct for the missing letters below?

The capt_ _ _ of detectives searched the kitch_ _ for a weap_ _. He had reas_ _ to believe the victims had been pois_ _ed. A pound of bac_ _, a leg of mutt_ _, a gall_ _ of water, a package of rais_ _s, and ev_ _ a ripe mel_ _ were sent to the lab for analysis.

COMPOUND WORDS

A Try to form as many **compound words** as possible. Combine words in column **A** with those in column **B**. You may use words more than once.

A	B
birth	body
flash	mobile
grand	walk
other	snake
snow	nut
some	ever
home	ball
ice	berg
tooth	hike
view	ache
worth	daughter
what	while
up	work
volley	where
team	place
rattle	free
side	wise
no	thing
head	light
every	mate
dough	brush
care	point
hitch	roar

CONTRACTIONS

A Rewrite each sentence with **contractions** formed from the underlined words.

1. You should not make up your mind until you have seen all the items.
2. If they had not forgotten their skates they would be able with us.
3. We had better leave now since it will soon be getting dark.
4. I do not remember who is in charge of picking up the supplies.
5. That is the third time she has not been able to meet with us.

B Write the full version of the following contractions:

haven't	where's
here's	you'd
mustn't	here's
he'd	you've
they'll	I'd

PLURALS

Regular nouns and nouns ending in s, sh, ch, and x

A Change the following singular nouns to their plural forms.

message	actress	sandwich
stranger	speech	prefix
toothbrush	promise	compass
scratch	ski	circus
reflex	branch	eyelash
octopus	address	change

Nouns ending with y

B Remember there are different patterns depending on whether the **y** is preceded by a *vowel* or a *consonant*.

1. Try making each of the following nouns plural.

chimney	journey	country
allergy	turkey	trophy
kidney	enemy	library
sky	valley	century
city	attorney	monkey
luxury	policy	donkey

Nouns ending with o, f, or fe

C Most nouns ending with **o**, **f**, or **fe** form the plural by adding **s**.

1. Make the following nouns plural, remembering that some of the exceptions are included in the list.

banjo	belief	rodeo
giraffe	hero	knife
studio	video	sheriff
dwarf	tomato	wife
roof	echo	life
potato	piano	wolf

D The nouns below all reflect special plural forms.

1. Can you change each noun below to its plural form?

child	cupful	crisis
medium	diagnosis	woman
handful	man	analysis
hypothesis	teaspoonful	datum

POSSESSIVES

A Convert the phrases to the possessive form.

1. the book belonging to the child
2. the diaper belonging to the baby
3. the decision of the referee
4. the account of the witness
5. the verdict of the judges
6. the equipment belonging to the players
7. the complaints of the citizens
8. the cries of the babies
9. the toys made by the elves
10. the testimony of the witnesses
11. the laughter of the children
12. the clothing of the men

ADDING ENDINGS: Y TO I

A Remember the patterns for adding endings to words ending in a **consonant + y**, as in **satisfy**:

- *keep* the **final y** when adding a suffix beginning with the letter i;
- *change* the **y to i** when adding all other suffixes.

1. Complete the following by adding –*ed* and –*ing* to the base word.

Base word (verb)	–*ed*	–*ing*
supply	_____	_____
occupy	_____	_____
bury	_____	_____
pity	_____	_____
justify	_____	_____

2. Supply the correct form of the verb in brackets.

a) (**testify**) The witness _____ at the trial yesterday.

b) (**marry**) Is he _____ the girl we met last month?

c) (**multiply**) The gerbils _____ in their cage overnight!

d) (**satisfy**) Are you _____ that you have the answer?

e) (**rely**) The team is _____ on your leadership.

3. Add the suffixes to the base words, making any necessary changes to the base word.

Base word	Suffix =	New word
glory	–ous	_____
lonely	–ness	_____
heavy	–ly	_____
funny	–est	_____
lucky	–ly	_____
clumsy	–ness	_____
envy	–ous	_____
magnify	–ed	_____
costly	–est	_____
fury	–ous	_____

ADDING ENDINGS:
WORDS ENDING IN SILENT E

A Remember the patterns for adding suffixes to words ending in **silent e**, such as **achieve**:

- *drop* the **silent e** when adding a suffix beginning with a vowel or y (**approve + al = approval**);
- *keep* the **silent e** when adding a suffix beginning with a consonant (**arrange + ment = arrangement**).

1. Match the suffixes to the base words, making any necessary changes to the base word.

Base word	Suffix =	New word
propose	–al	_____
announce	–ment	_____
write	–ing	_____
juice	–y	_____
vary	–ous	_____
mercy	–ful	_____
encourage	–ing	_____
encourage	–ment	_____
value	–able	_____
achieve	–ment	_____

2. Now try to complete the following sentences with the correct form of the word in brackets.

   a) (**guide**) We asked the _____ counsellor to help us solve our problem.

   b) (**absolute**) That rumour is _____ false.

c) (continue) Are you _____ to have problems with your knee?

d) (qualify) Eric _____ for the finals in tomorrow's swimming trials.

e) (mystery) What is that _____ noise coming from the attic?

f) (advertise) Did you see the _____ for our sale in the newspaper?

g) (pity) Our poor dog Max looked _____ as he stood in the rain.

h) (hope) I was _____ you could stay for awhile.

i) (fame) His uncle is a _____ scientist.

j) (steady) It was raining _____ the day of the picnic.

3. The following words are exceptions. Do you know them?

Base word	Suffix =	New word
notice	–able	_____
argue	–ment	_____
double	–ly	_____
courage	–ous	_____
nine	–th	_____
true	–ly	_____
outrage	–ous	_____
twelve	–th	_____
awe	–ful	_____
wide	–th	_____

ADDING ENDINGS:
DOUBLING BEFORE SUFFIXES

A Add a suffix to the word in brackets:

1. (**cram**) My brother's closet is _____ full of dirty clothes.
2. (**slam**) The car _____ into the tree at the end of the lane.
3. (**jump**) The children were _____ up and down with delight.
4. (**fit**) The jigsaw puzzle is finally _____ together.
5. (**slip**) We had great fun _____ and sliding on the ice.

B Now add the suffix *–ed* and *–ing* to each verb. Some of the base words will require doubling the final consonants, while others will stay the same. Listen for the stressed syllable as a clue for doubling.

Base word (verb)	–ed	–ing
refer	_____	_____
listen	_____	_____
omit	_____	_____
equip	_____	_____
pardon	_____	_____
patrol	_____	_____
occur	_____	_____
pilot	_____	_____
prefer	_____	_____
happen	_____	_____

OTHER DOUBLING PATTERNS

A Each of the following words has a double letter pattern. Focus on these letters as you write the words. You may wish to circle the double letters, write them in a different colour, or highlight them in some other way to help you remember them.

a_ _ident	mi_ _pelled	i_ _ortal
ba_ _el	su_ _estion	nece_ _ary
c_ – _perate	o_ _ur	su_ _e_ _ful
vani_ _a	para_ _el	sheri _ _
o_ _asional	su_ _ound	a_ _ountant
a_ _earance	r_ _lect	i_ _ediately
i_ _igation	penici_ _in	va_ _inate
profe_ _ion	stu_ _orn	squi_ _el
o_ _ortunity	a_ _reciate	u_ _atural
su_ _ender	magica_ _y	cha_ _enge

RELATED WORDS

A Remember this important principle of our English spelling system:

> Words which are related in *meaning* are usually related in *spelling*—even if they do not sound the same.

1. Use the form of the base word as a clue to the correct spelling of the related form.

Base word	Related form
admire	adm_ration
bomb	bom_ard
column	colum_ist
condemn	condem_ation
confide	conf_dent
define	def_nition
design	desi_nation
excel	exc_llent
expose	exp_sition
install	inst_llation
invite	inv_tation
moist	mois_en
muscle	mus_ular
oblige	obl_gation
oppose	opp_sition
resign	resi_nation
resolve	res_lution

2. Complete each of these sentences with the base form in brackets.

a) (**violate**) He was fined $100 for the traffic _____.

b) (**operate**) The _____ on her knee is scheduled for today.

c) (**ignite**) There seems to be a problem with the car's _____ system.

d) (**produce**) The _____ of steel involves several processes.

e) (**receive**) We have an invitation to the wedding _____.

f) (**athlete**) She has a great deal of _____ ability.

g) (**nation**) An inter_____ track meet is being held in Vancouver next month.

h) (**oblige**) You are under no _____ to purchase this product.

i) (**private**) The fence was built to ensure the _____ of the residents.

j) (**major**) The _____ of the students is in favour of having the performance.

HOMOPHONES

A *Witch won due ewe no?* Select the correct **homophone** in brackets to complete each sentence.

1. (**wait, weight**) If you can _____ a moment I will check your _____ on the scales.

2. (**chilly, chili**) There is nothing as good as a warm bowl of _____ on a _____ winter's night.

3. (**aloud, allowed**) You are not _____ to say the answer _____ until everyone has finished.

4. (**seen, scene**) The accused was _____ near the _____ of the accident.

5. (**week, weak**) Ever since last _____ I have been feeling tired and _____.

6. (**vein, vain**) The nurse tried in _____ to find a _____ in the patient's arm.

7. (**scent, sent**) My favourite _____ of perfume was _____ to me by my boyfriend.

8. (**board, bored**) Don't you ever become _____ with skate_____ing?

9. (**died, dyed**) I almost _____ when I saw the colour she had _____ her hair!

10. (**fare, fair**) Do you think it was _____ that we were asked to pay the taxi _____?

11. (**threw, through**) They _____ the paper airplanes _____ the doorway.

12. (**herd, heard**) I thought I _____ you say that a _____ of cows was in the pasture.

13. (**There, Their**) _____ jackets must be in the pile over _____.

14. (**pain, pane**) She was in great _____ after she cut her arm on the broken _____ of glass.

15. (**to, too, two**) I would like _____ order _____ copies of that book, _____ please.

Bibliography

Spelling

Henderson, E. (1985). *Teaching Spelling.* Boston: Houghton Mifflin Company.

Scott, R. & Siamon, S. (1989). *Canadian Spelling Program II, 4-6.* Toronto: Gage Educational Publishing Company.

Suid, M. (1981). *Demonic Mnemonics*. California: David S. Lake Pub.

Tarasoff, M. (1990). *Spelling: Strategies You Can Teach.* Victoria: Pixelart Graphics.

Thomas, V. (1979). *Teaching Spelling.* Toronto: Gage Educational Publishing Company.

Word Games

Brandreth, G. (1980). *The Joy of Lex: How to Have Fun with 860,341,500 Words.* New York: William Morrow.

Daniel, B. (1988). *Spelling Thinkercises.* Carthage, Il.: Good Apple Inc.

Daniel, B. (1988). *Word Thinkercises.* Carthage, Il.: Good Apple Inc.

Golick, M. (1989). *Playing with Words.* Markham, Ontario: Pembroke Books.

Kohl, H. (1981). *A Book of Puzzlements: Play and Invention with Language.* New York: Schocken Books.

Moscovitch, R. (1985). *What's in a Word? A Dictionary of Daffy Definitions.* Boston: Houghton Mifflin Co.

Word Lists

Moore, G. (1988). *Heath Wordfinder.* Lexington: D.C. Heath.

Fry, E. (1985). *The New Reading Teacher's Book of Lists.* Englewood Cliffs: Prentice-Hall.

Word Origins

Freeman, E. (1985). *The Story Behind the Word.* Philadelphia: ISI Press.

Glazier, T. (1985). *The Least You Should Know about Vocabulary Building.* New York: Holt, Rinehart & Winston.

Hoad, T. (1986). *The Concise Oxford Dictionary of English Etymology.* Oxford: Oxford University Press.

McConnell, R. (1979). *Our Own Voice.* Toronto: Gage Educational Publishing Company.

Dictionaries and Thesauruses

Avis, Walter S., et al. (1979). *Gage Intermediate Dictionary.* Toronto: Gage Educational Publishing Company.

Avis, Walter S., et al. (1983). *Gage Canadian Dictionary.* Toronto: Gage Educational Publishing Company.

Knight, Linsay, ed. (1988). *Young Canada Thesaurus.* Toronto: Nelson Canada.

Index